WHAT'S YOUR WORLDVIEW?

# WHAT'S YOUR WORLDVIEW?

AN INTERACTIVE APPROACH
TO LIFE'S BIG QUESTIONS

JAMES N. ANDERSON

**::CROSSWAY**®
WHEATON, ILLINOIS

*What's Your Worldview? An Interactive Approach to Life's Big Questions*
Copyright © 2014 by James N. Anderson

Published by Crossway
    1300 Crescent Street
    Wheaton, Illinois 60187

All rights reserved. No part of this publication may be reproduced, stored in a retrieval system, or transmitted in any form by any means, electronic, mechanical, photocopy, recording, or otherwise, without the prior permission of the publisher, except as provided for by USA copyright law. Crossway® is a registered trademark in the United States of America.

Cover design: Tyler Deeb, Pedale Design

First printing 2013

Printed in the United States of America

Scripture quotations are from the ESV® Bible (The Holy Bible, English Standard Version®), copyright © 2001 by Crossway. 2011 Text Edition. Used by permission. All rights reserved.

Trade paperback ISBN: 978-1-4335-3892-6
Mobipocket ISBN: 978-1-4335-3894-0
PDF ISBN: 978-1-4335-3893-3
ePub ISBN: 978-1-4335-3895-7

---

**Library of Congress Cataloging-in-Publication Data**
Anderson, James N., 1973–
  What's your worldview? : an interactive approach to life's big questions / James N. Anderson.
    pages cm.
  Includes bibliographical references and index.
  ISBN 978-1-4335-3892-6 (tp)
  1. Philosophy—Miscellanea. 2. Religions—Miscellanea.
I. Title.
BD21.A53      2014
100—dc23                            2013018450

---

Crossway is a publishing ministry of Good News Publishers.

| VP | | 24 | 23 | 22 | 21 | 20 | 19 | 18 | 17 | 16 |
|----|----|----|----|----|----|----|----|----|----|----|
| 17 | 16 | 15 | 14 | 13 | 12 | 11 | 10 | 9  | 8  | 7  |

To John Frame

# Contents

Introduction                                                      11

Part I
## QUESTIONS

The Freedom Question                                              19
The Truth Question                                                21
The Knowledge Question                                            22
The Goodness Question                                             23
The Religion Question                                             24
The God Question                                                  25
The Unity Question                                                26
The Matter Question                                               27
The Mind Question                                                 28
The Personality Question                                          29
The All-Is-God Question                                           30
The All-In-God Question                                           31
The Perfection Question                                           32
The Uniqueness Question                                           33
The Communication Question                                        34
The Openness Question                                             35
The Resurrection Question                                         36
The Muhammad Question                                             37
The Moses Question                                                38
The Divinity Question                                             39
The Salvation Question                                            40

## Part II
# CATEGORIES

| | |
|---|---|
| Atheist Worldviews | 43 |
| Theist Worldviews | 45 |
| Quasi-Theist Worldviews | 47 |
| Finite Theist Worldviews | 49 |
| Non-Christian Theist Worldviews | 51 |

## Part III
# WORLDVIEWS

| | |
|---|---|
| Worldview: Atheistic Dualism | 55 |
| Worldview: Atheistic Idealism | 57 |
| Worldview: Christianity | 59 |
| Worldview: Deism | 61 |
| Worldview: Finite Godism | 63 |
| Worldview: Islam | 65 |
| Worldview: Judaism | 67 |
| Worldview: Materialism | 69 |
| Worldview: Monism | 71 |
| Worldview: Mysticism | 73 |
| Worldview: Nihilism | 75 |
| Worldview: Non-Mainstream Monotheism | 77 |
| Worldview: Panentheism | 79 |
| Worldview: Pantheism | 81 |
| Worldview: Pelagianism | 83 |
| Worldview: Platonism | 85 |
| Worldview: Pluralism | 87 |
| Worldview: Polytheism | 89 |
| Worldview: Relativism | 91 |
| Worldview: Skepticism | 93 |
| Worldview: Unitarianism | 95 |

| | |
|---|---|
| Appendix: Questions and Answers | 97 |
| Notes | 105 |
| Subject Index | 109 |

# Introduction

Have you ever read one of the "Choose Your Own Adventure" (CYOA) books? The basic idea behind them is ingenious. Rather than telling a story from a traditional third-person perspective, with a linear storyline and a pre-determined ending, a CYOA book has an "interactive storyline" in which the reader acts as the main character and determines the plot by making decisions at key points. CYOA books are sometimes called "game books" because reading one is like playing a game. Each book has many possible endings—some happy, some not so happy—but the outcome always depends crucially on *your* choices.

For example, on one page of a CYOA book you might find a belligerent goblin standing in your way. Do you try to flatter him into letting you pass or do you use the mysterious magic potion you picked up on page 12? If you choose the flattery strategy, you turn to page 22; if the potion, you turn instead to page 31. On one of these two pages, the adventure continues unabated. On the other page, things pan out a whole lot better for the hook-nosed green dude than for you. (Now you're dying to know which page was which. Exciting stuff, isn't it?)

This book is similar to a "Choose Your Own Adventure" book in some ways and very different in other ways. The similarity is that it's not meant to be read sequentially from cover to cover. (Please don't try to do that—you'll find it very confusing!) Instead, you're invited to make key decisions or choices at a number of points in order to determine the outcome. It's not really a "game book," but there's still a sense in which you're a "player." How things turn out in the end really depends on *you*.

I'll be the first to admit that this book may not be quite as exciting and entertaining as a CYOA book, but it deals with something far more important—one might even say *infinitely* more important. I hope you'll agree once you get into it. In this book, rather than choosing an adventure, you'll end up choosing a *worldview*.

## What in the World Is a Worldview?

You may have come across the word *worldview* before, but don't be put off if you haven't. I'll try to define the term clearly and explain why it's such an important concept.

Just as the word itself suggests, a worldview is an overall view of the world. It's not a *physical* view of the world, like the sight of planet Earth you might get from an orbiting space station. Rather, it's a *philosophical* view of the world—and not just of our planet, but of all of reality. A worldview is an all-encompassing perspective on everything that exists and matters to us.

Your worldview represents your most fundamental beliefs and assumptions about the universe you inhabit. It reflects how you would answer all the "big questions" of human existence, the fundamental questions we ask about life, the universe, and everything.

Is there a God? If so, what is God like and how do I relate to God? If there isn't a God, does it matter? What is truth and can anyone really know the truth anyway? Where did the universe come from and where is it going—if anywhere? What's the meaning of life? Does my life have a purpose—and, if so, what is it? What am I supposed to do with my life? What does it mean to live a *good* life? Does it really matter in the end whether or not I live a good life? Is there life after death? Are humans basically just smart apes with superior hygiene and fashion sense—or is there more to us than that?

You get the idea. Your worldview directly influences how you answer those kinds of big questions—or how you *would* answer them if you were asked and gave them some thought.

Worldviews are like belly buttons. Everyone has one, but we don't talk about them very often. Or perhaps it would be better to say that worldviews are like cerebellums: everyone has one and we can't live without them, but not everyone *knows* that he has one.

A worldview is as indispensable for thinking as an atmosphere is for breathing. You can't think in an intellectual vacuum any more than you can breathe without a physical atmosphere. Most of the time, you take the atmosphere around you for granted: you look *through* it rather than *at* it, even though you know it's always there. Much the same goes for your worldview: normally you look through it rather than directly at it. It's essential, but it usually sits in the background of your thought.

Your worldview shapes and informs your experiences of the world around you. Like a pair of spectacles with colored lenses, it affects what you see and how you see it. Depending on the "color" of the lenses, you see some things more easily, while other things are de-emphasized or distorted. In some cases, you don't see things at all.

Here are a few examples to illustrate how your worldview affects the way you see things. Suppose that one day a close friend tells you that she recently met with a spiritualist who put her in touch with a loved one who died ten years ago. Later that day, you read an article about a statue of the Virgin Mary that witnesses claim to have seen weeping blood. You also hear a news story on the radio about possible signs of complex organic life discovered on Mars. Your worldview—your background assumptions about God, the origin and nature of the universe, human beginnings, life after death, and so forth—strongly influences how you interpret these reports and react to them.

Worldviews also largely determine people's opinions on matters of ethics and politics. What you think about abortion, euthanasia, same-sex relationships, public education, economic policy, foreign aid, the use of military force, environmentalism, animal rights, genetic enhancement, and almost any other major issue of the day depends on your underlying worldview more than anything else.

As you can see, then, worldviews play a central and defining role in our lives. They shape what we believe and what we're willing to believe, how we interpret our experiences, how we behave in response to those experiences, and how we relate to others.

I hope by now you have a good sense of what a worldview is and why it's so significant. As I said earlier, this book is about choosing a

Introduction

worldview rather than choosing an adventure (although I like to think there's something quite adventurous about reflecting deeply on all the big questions). Strictly speaking, however, in this book you're not so much *choosing* a worldview as *identifying* your worldview, because you already have a worldview, even if you don't realize it. So one of the purposes of this book is to help you identify and clarify your worldview and its implications.

Nevertheless, what you read here may also prompt you to reconsider your worldview—perhaps even to change it. It isn't easy for someone to change his or her worldview—it can be like relocating to another continent, intellectually speaking—but it can and does happen. For example, the novelist C. S. Lewis famously moved from an Atheist worldview to a Theist worldview, partly through discussions with his colleague and friend J. R. R. Tolkien. But even if you stick with your current worldview, this book will give you the opportunity to explore a number of alternative worldviews, all of which are (or have been) held by real people at some time and place.

Here are the main goals of this book:

- To help you identify and clarify your worldview.
- To encourage you to consider the big questions and to think through some of the implications of various answers.
- To help you appreciate that there are important differences between worldviews—and that not all worldviews are created equal! (I'll say more about this last point in a moment.)

## How Does the Book Work?

You'll be presented with a series of questions that are designed to be answered yes or no. (Don't worry if you're not really sure how to answer a particular question. Just go with the answer that best reflects your current beliefs, the answer that seems to you most likely to be true. You can always go back and choose a different answer later if you want to.) The question will be stated in a box at the top of the page, and the rest of the page will give an explanation of the question to make sure you understand exactly what you're being asked.

Depending on your answer to the question, you'll be directed to another page, where you'll find one of the following:

- A further question, to narrow down the remaining options.
- A brief commentary on your answer and its implications.
- A final worldview page.

The last of these will have "Worldview" in the page heading. If you land on one of these pages, you've hit the end of the trail you have followed. There you'll find a summary of the type of worldview you have based on all the answers you gave, along with some commentary designed to provoke further thought. You'll also have the option to go back up the trail, so to speak, by returning to one of the earlier question pages.

As I mentioned at the beginning, one of the features of a "Choose Your Own Adventure" book is that not all of the possible storylines have happy endings. Often a poor choice leads to a short and sticky end. Your choices have consequences—sometimes fatal consequences! In a manner of speaking, the same goes for the different outcomes in this book. Some worldviews have more serious problems than others. Some walk with a pronounced limp. Some have failing organs. Some are mortally wounded. A few are simply "dead on arrival"! In each case, I'll point out a few of these problems, but I'll leave it to you to make the final diagnosis and prognosis.

Let's go back to the encounter with the goblin for a moment. In fact, going back is exactly what you would do, I suspect, if you made a poor choice the first time you met the goblin. I know I would! If I got squished, I'd flip back to the earlier page and take a different path. I'm pretty sure that's what most readers of CYOA books do when their stories come to abrupt and undesirable ends. Is that cheating? Not at all. It's just getting your money's worth from the book!

I want to encourage you to approach this book in much the same way. If you don't like the outcome of your answers to the questions, please feel free to flip back to the previous question, or to an even earlier one, and follow a *different* path. I want you to get your money's

## Introduction

worth! In fact, I hope you'll be intrigued enough to explore *every* path in the book, along with the worldviews at the ends of all those paths, because that will help you to gain an even better understanding of your own worldview.

There's one other issue I should mention before we get started. Since everyone has a worldview, I have my own worldview, too, of course. I'm not going to tell you which worldview that is, but I haven't tried to disguise it. You should be able to figure it out by exploring the different "storylines" in the book and reflecting on my comments on each worldview.

Does that mean the whole book is biased? Well, sure! But if you think about it, that's unavoidable. Since everyone has a worldview, everyone has a bias. All of us are naturally biased toward our own worldviews, and all of us tend to interpret and evaluate the world in accordance with our worldviews. So do I have a bias? Yes, of course—but so do you!

The real issue isn't whether we have biases—we all do—but whether we're aware of them and able to think critically about them. In a certain sense, each of us can step into someone else's worldview, just as we can step into someone else's house, to examine it "from the inside" and to compare it with our own. I've tried to represent other worldviews fairly in this book: to summarize them accurately and to be realistic about their strengths and weaknesses. Even if you think I've failed in some cases, I hope you will nonetheless learn something useful along the way and benefit from thinking about these important matters.

No doubt this book will raise a number of questions in your mind. I've tried to anticipate the most common questions and provide answers in the appendix (page 97).

Well, that's more than enough introduction!

Are you ready to begin the "adventure"? If so, just turn the page.

Part I

# QUESTIONS

# The Freedom Question

> DO YOU HAVE THE POWER TO MAKE *FREE* CHOICES?

Chips or salad? Diet Coke or Dr Pepper? Dine-in or take-out?

It's a basic fact of human life that we make choices. We make them all the time—sometimes so effortlessly and so subtly that we don't even notice it. For example, you chose to start reading this book. By continuing to read it, you're implicitly choosing not to do something else right now. Before this day is over, you'll make hundreds more choices.

But are those choices *free*? That's one of the most enduring questions in the history of human thought. Some philosophers have said that we do make free choices, while others have denied it. Still others have said that our choices are free in some senses but not free in others.

There's a sense in which even a computer makes choices. For instance, it chooses the best time to run maintenance services (usually when the computer is idle). Nevertheless, we don't usually think of a computer as making *free* choices, the kind of choices that are made by a thoughtful, self-conscious, morally responsible agent. It's just a machine following its programming.

But what about *you*? Are your choices just the stimulus-response outputs of a neurological computer (also known as your brain)? Or are they the free choices of a morally responsible agent?

Do you have the power to make *free* choices?

**If you answered yes to the Freedom Question, go to page 20.**
**If you answered no to the Freedom Question, go to page 20.**

# A Joke with a Serious Point

Forgive me! I couldn't resist beginning with a little philosophical humor. As you probably realized, you were directed to this page no matter how you answered the Freedom Question.

But there's a serious point here, too. One of our most basic human intuitions is that we, unlike computers and robots, have the ability to make free choices in life: to deliberate about our options and to select between different courses of action. What's more, we're often held morally responsible for our choices (and rightly so). You may be reading this book simply for entertainment, but how you decide to answer the questions, and how you respond to what you subsequently read, is, in a very important sense, *up to you*. And how you choose to respond may well have important implications for your life and the lives of others.

So press on! Consider carefully how you would answer the questions and take responsibility for the choices you make and their implications for your worldview.

Of course, some readers of this book may still want to insist that in reality none of us make any free choices and none of us are morally responsible for our choices, despite our strong intuitions to the contrary. If that's what you really think, it's going to be difficult to change your mind at this point.

But on one level, that doesn't matter for the purposes of this book. After all, you've already made the choices to pick up the book and to read this far, even if those weren't *free* choices. In the same way, you can choose to *continue* to read: to answer the questions and to reflect further on your worldview.

For the time being, I'm happy to settle for that.

**Now continue to page 21.**

# The Truth Question

> IS THERE *ANY* OBJECTIVE TRUTH?

"It's all relative, isn't it?"

Some people believe—or at least claim to believe—that all truth is relative. They say that what's true for one person need not be true for another person, or that what's true for people in one culture (e.g., a Jewish community in New York) needn't be true for people in another culture (e.g., a Buddhist community in Tibet). Such folk often insist that truth isn't something "out there" to be discovered; rather, truth is something we choose or create for ourselves. Truth is always "inside" us rather than "outside" us.

So, for example, while the statement "There is a God" may be true for some people, it doesn't have to be true for everyone. What's true is always *relative* to a person's particular viewpoint, context, or culture. So we shouldn't speak about *the* truth, as though truth is the same for everyone. Rather, we should speak about *my* truth, *your* truth, *their* truth, and so on.

In contrast, other people insist that many truths—including the most important truths—are *objectively* true. There are some things that are just true period, regardless of what anyone happens to think, hope, or feel about those matters. (As they sometimes say, "The truth hurts!") These objective truths are true for everyone, everywhere, because they're based on objective facts about reality that are independent of human ideas, desires, and feelings. According to this view, it makes no sense to say that the statement "There is a God" could be true for me but not true for you. Either it's true or it isn't: end of story.

But which position do you take? Is there *any* objective truth?

**If you answered yes to the Truth Question, go to page 22.**
**If you answered no to the Truth Question, go to page 91.**

# The Knowledge Question

> IS IT POSSIBLE TO *KNOW* THE TRUTH?

It's little use having millions of dollars in the bank if you can't *access* that money. In the same way, objective truth is little use to us if we can't *access* it—if we can't know, with some degree of confidence, just what that truth is. If the truth is unknowable, if it's always beyond our grasp, there might as well be no truth at all. We'd be wasting our time by trying to pursue it.

Most people would agree that we have intellectual faculties, such as reason and perception, that allow us to investigate matters of interest to us and to discover the truth about those matters. Even if we don't have absolute certainty about most things, we can still know a great deal about ourselves and the world around us by using our intellectual faculties in responsible ways. For example, most educated folk would say they know that Mount Everest is the highest peak in the world, even though, strictly speaking, it's possible to be mistaken about something like that.

Other people, however, take a much lower view of the human mind. They insist that even if there is objective truth about important matters, no one can really know what it is. Everyone has his own opinions, and some of those opinions may happen to be true, but no one's opinions are more or less reasonable than anyone else's. Certainly no one has any right to say she *knows* the truth. We're all mired in ignorance, and the sooner we accept that the better.

Which side do you take on this issue? Is it possible to *know* the truth—at least *some* truth?

**If you answered yes to the Knowledge Question, go to page 23.**
**If you answered no to the Knowledge Question, go to page 93.**

# The Goodness Question

> IS ANYTHING *OBJECTIVELY* GOOD OR BAD?

"That was a good meal!" "Bush was a bad president." "I'm sure you did the right thing." "Abortion is always wrong." "Osama bin Laden was an evil man." "The invasion of Iraq wasn't justified."

All of these statements involve value judgments of some kind or another. They don't simply state facts in a disinterested way; rather, they make evaluations of the facts. They make judgments that certain things are "good" or "bad," "right" or "wrong," "justified" or "unjustified."

All of us make value judgments all the time. Some are very significant, others not so much. Either way, value judgments are an essential feature of human life.

But is anything *objectively* valuable? Is anything *objectively* good in the sense that it is a good thing *period*, regardless of what anyone happens to think, hope, or feel about it?

Some people believe that all value judgments are ultimately relative or subjective, that they're no more than expressions of human preferences, either personal preferences or cultural preferences. On this view, nothing is *intrinsically* good or bad. Instead, we *make* things valuable by projecting our desires, tastes, and goals onto the world.

Other people insist that some things—such as marital love and musical skill—are *objectively* good, while other things—such as rape and child abuse—are *objectively* bad. Their goodness or badness isn't ultimately a matter of personal or cultural preferences.

Which view do you take? Is anything *objectively* good or bad?

**If you answered yes to the Goodness Question, go to page 24.**
**If you answered no to the Goodness Question, go to page 75.**

# The Religion Question

> IS THERE MORE THAN ONE VALID RELIGION?

There's a bewildering diversity of religion in our world, and we're more aware of it than ever. Encyclopedias are devoted to documenting the ever-increasing number of religious faiths and ideologies, some of which are quite obscure. By most estimates, there are around twenty religions (or families of religions) that have more than one million adherents. Whatever else you might think about religion, it's clear that humans have a natural religious impulse.

But what do we make of this diversity? Some simply insist that all religions are misguided. (Atheists usually take this view.) Others want to say that *at most* one religion can be valid. For example, Christians often claim that Christianity is the only true religion, while Muslims say the same for Islam, and so forth.

An increasingly popular view, however, is that *more than one* religion can be valid. According to this view, Hinduism is right for some people; Buddhism works for other people; Judaism for still others; and so on. By the same logic, some people might not be suited to any religion at all.

On this way of thinking, the different religions represent diverse but equally valid perspectives on the ultimate reality. Sometimes the analogy is used of a group of blind men encountering an elephant. One feels the trunk and says, "It's like a snake!" Finding a tusk, another says, "It's like a spear!" A third grasps the tail and says, "It's like a rope!" The conclusions are vastly different, but none of them is more or less right than the others. Each man interprets the whole according to his own individual (and limited) perspective. So the major world religions, some argue, are like those men feeling the elephant.

Do you agree? Is there more than one valid religion?

**If you answered yes to the Religion Question, go to page 87.**
**If you answered no to the Religion Question, go to page 25.**

# The God Question

IS THERE A GOD?

This is the big one. You knew it was coming. The God Question is undoubtedly one of the most important questions to ask, because it marks a major fork in the road when it comes to worldviews. How you answer the God Question has enormous implications for how you understand yourself, your relation to others, and your place in the universe. Remarkably, however, many people in the West today don't give this question nearly the attention it deserves; they live as though it doesn't really matter to everyday life. As the rest of this book will show, that kind of indifference is a big mistake.

But what exactly is this question asking? What precisely do we mean by "God"? Definitions are crucial here, because often people who claim to believe in God have very different conceptions of God.

For the purposes of this question, and to keep things relatively simple for now, let's define "God" in fairly broad terms. We can nail down the details later on, such as whether God is a personal being, whether God has communicated with human beings, and whether there is only one God.

So here's our question spelled out more precisely: Is there a Supreme Being that deserves our worship and gives meaning, purpose, and direction to the universe and to human life? (If you think more than one being meets this description, you should answer yes to the God Question for now.)

**If you answered yes to the God Question, go to page 45.**
**If you answered no to the God Question, go to page 43.**

# The Unity Question

> IS EVERYTHING ULTIMATELY ONE?

What did the Buddhist say to the hot dog vendor? "Make me one with everything."

It's an old joke—and a pretty lame one, too—but lurking behind it is one of the most enduring philosophical issues of all time. It's essentially a question of *counting*. Ultimately, how many distinct things are there? Is there really only one thing or are there many things? Is the universe an indivisible unity? Or is it divisible into more fundamental parts or constituents, such as atomic particles?

The ancient Greek philosopher Parmenides (ca. 500 BC) insisted that everything is indeed ultimately one. At the most fundamental level, there is only one being, one existent thing—which Parmenides imaginatively referred to as "the One." (If you've seen the movie *The Matrix*, try not to picture Keanu Reeves at this point.) According to Parmenides, everything that has real existence is ultimately identical with the One. It is a pure, infinite, indivisible unity, and there is nothing else but the One.

Parmenides doesn't stand alone in his answer to the Unity Question. (Well, unless he was *right*, of course!) A few other philosophers have sided with him, but most have taken the opposite view, that there is more than one thing in reality. The apparent diversity in the world is real. It's not a mere illusion.

Whose side do *you* take? Is everything ultimately one?

**If you answered yes to the Unity Question, go to page 71.**
**If you answered no to the Unity Question, go to page 27.**

# The Matter Question

> IS EVERYTHING ULTIMATELY MATERIAL IN NATURE?

Your answers to the God Question and the Unity Question indicate that you hold an Atheist worldview but not a Monist worldview (see page 71). You think there are ultimately many distinct things in the universe, but none of those things is God (in any traditional sense of the term *God*).

But what *kind* of things are there? What is their essential nature?

Philosophers have often acknowledged two basic categories of things: *material* things and *mental* things. Material things consist of physical matter or energy. They exist in space, they have size and shape, they can be perceived with our senses, and they causally interact with one another in regular, predictable, law-like ways. Some examples would be your brain, your cell phone, the Golden Gate Bridge, and the moons of Jupiter.

Mental things, on the other hand, don't have a size and shape in space, they can't be perceived with our senses, and they aren't governed by the laws of physics. Some examples would be your mind, your feelings about a beloved pet, your memories of your childhood, your plans for tomorrow, and your thoughts as you read this book.

The question before you now is this: Is *everything* that exists ultimately a *material* thing? Are there *only* material things in the final analysis? Is everything reducible to matter and energy?

Of course, your answer might be that *some* things are material in nature but *other* things are not, and those other things can't be explained in terms of material things alone. In that case, your answer to the Matter Question should be no.

**If you answered yes to the Matter Question, go to page 69.**
**If you answered no to the Matter Question, go to page 28.**

# The Mind Question

> IS EVERYTHING ULTIMATELY MENTAL IN NATURE?

We've established that you're not a Materialist (see page 69). Many would say that's a good thing, because Materialism is a very impoverished, problematic, and depressing worldview. You likely answered no to the Matter Question because you realize that there are some things, such as our minds and the contents of our minds, that cannot be denied or explained away in purely material terms. It's hard to deny that our minds and our mental lives are real. After all, one needs a mind to even *think* about the question!

So not *everything* is material in nature. But is *anything* material in nature? Surprising as it may seem, some philosophers have denied that matter really exists, even though we appear to perceive material things. They have argued either that the very idea of matter is incoherent or that we don't need it to explain any of our experiences. All we need to explain our experiences is the idea that there are individual minds—your mind, my mind, and so on—that have experiences and thoughts of a material world that *appears* to exist in space and time.

According to these philosophers, everything that exists is ultimately *mental* in nature. Strictly speaking, the things we commonly describe as "material"—trees, rocks, birds, the stars, our bodies—exist only in our minds, as ideas or sensations. Nothing exists outside of minds. Nothing exists apart from minds. There's really no such thing as matter—only minds.

So *they* think. But what is *your* mind on the matter? Is everything ultimately mental in nature?

**If you answered yes to the Mind Question, go to page 57.**
**If you answered no to the Mind Question, go to page 55.**

# The Personality Question

> IS GOD A PERSONAL BEING?

Theist worldviews hold in common the belief that there is a God. However, the differences between the various Theist worldviews are extremely significant. It's one thing to say that there is a God. It's another thing to say what that God is *like*. People who say they believe in God can have very diverse understandings of "God." What's more, your conception of God has significant implications for your understanding of the universe, human beings, and your own nature and place in the universe.

So how can we narrow things down? One of the most basic questions we can ask about the nature of God is simply this: Is God a *personal* being?

We all have a basic understanding of what it means to be "personal." A person has the capacity for conscious thought and experience, including *self*-consciousness (the ability to reflect directly on one's own thoughts and experiences). A person can have intelligent thoughts, can have goals and plans, and can make free choices between different courses of action. We also often think of a person as having emotions and affections.

Every human is a person, but there could be personal beings that aren't human. An angel, if angels exist, would be a non-human person. So would be some of the non-human life-forms in science fiction stories (e.g., the Vulcans and Klingons in the *Star Trek* series).

But what about God? Is God a personal being? (If you think there's more than one deity, just answer this form of the question: Are *the gods* personal beings?)

**If you answered yes to the Personality Question, go to page 32.**
**If you answered no to the Personality Question, go to page 47.**

# The All-Is-God Question

> IS THE UNIVERSE GOD?

Your answers so far indicate that you have a Quasi-Theist worldview. In your view, there is a God, but that God is not a *personal* being.

There are, however, different types of Quasi-Theist worldviews. One way to get at the differences between them is to think about the relationship between God and the universe. (By "universe," I mean the physical cosmos along with any spiritual entities, such as souls, spirits, or angels, if any such things exist and inhabit the cosmos.)

Some people say that the relationship between God and the universe is very simple: they're *identical*. God is the universe and the universe is God.

The seventeenth-century philosopher Baruch Spinoza took this view. In his writings, he referred to *Deus sive Natura*, which is Latin for "God or Nature." His point was that "God" and "Nature" are just different names for the same thing, and that thing is simply *everything*—the whole enchilada. There is nothing else but God, and God is the universe, the totality of physical and spiritual reality (which includes us, of course).

Since it's hard to think that the universe *as a whole* is a personal being (even if it *contains* personal beings like us), those who take this view are inclined to say that God is not a personal being.

But what's *your* view? Do you think the universe is God—that they're one and the same? Or do you think that God is *distinct* from the universe in some significant way?

**If you answered yes to the All-Is-God Question, go to page 81.**
**If you answered no to the All-Is-God Question, go to page 31.**

# The All-In-God Question

> IS THE UNIVERSE WITHIN GOD?

You answered no to the All-Is-God Question, which means you think that God isn't identical to the universe. Rather, God is *greater* than the universe. God, in some sense, is *beyond* the universe. (But this deity isn't a *personal* being; recall that you answered no to the Personality Question.)

If God and the universe aren't identical, there are at least a couple of other ways to understand their relationship. One option is that the universe is a *part* of God rather than the whole of God. God encompasses everything, but the universe isn't everything. The part isn't the whole, but it's *within* the whole.

One way to look at this is to suppose that the relationship between God and the universe is similar to the relationship between the soul and the body. You're not *identical* to your body—there's more to you than mere flesh and bones—but your body is certainly a *part* of you. (Who else would it belong to?) So you are the composite of a soul and a body. In a similar way, one might think that God is a composite of the physical universe and something else—an infinite and eternal soul, perhaps. So that's one possibility for a Quasi-Theist: the universe is a part of God.

The other option is that God is *completely distinct* from the universe: there is a non-personal Supreme Being that utterly transcends the universe. On this view, there's no "overlap" between God and the universe. The universe is distinct from God and subordinate to God.

So which of these two options do you think is correct? Is the universe within God or not?

**If you answered yes to the All-In-God Question, go to page 79.**
**If you answered no to the All-In-God Question, go to page 85.**

# The Perfection Question

> IS GOD A PERFECT BEING?

We're making good progress! We've established that you're a Theist of some kind. You believe that there is a God, a Supreme Being who is personal in nature and gives meaning, purpose, and direction to the universe. These beliefs fit very well with the answers you gave to the earlier Truth and Goodness Questions: there is objective truth and there is an objective standard of good and evil.

Now we need to narrow things down further by asking some more precise questions about your conception of God.

Most Theists consider God to be a *perfect* being. God is absolutely unsurpassable in every respect, has no flaws or external limitations, and is not dependent on anything or anyone else. God simply could not be better than he already is in any respect. A perfect God must be all-good, all-wise, all-knowing, and all-powerful, and that God must be the transcendent creator and sustainer of everything else that exists.

There are some Theists, however, who believe that God isn't a perfect being in every respect. They usually maintain that God is *morally* perfect, but they may argue that God is limited in his *knowledge* or in his *power* by other beings in the universe. They may even believe that God, like us, exists *within* the universe, subject to its limitations, rather than transcending the universe.

Where do you fall on that question? Is God a perfect being?

**If you answered yes to the Perfection Question, go to page 34.**
**If you answered no to the Perfection Question, go to page 49.**

# The Uniqueness Question

> IS THERE ONLY ONE GOD?

We've established that you hold to a Finite Theist worldview: you believe there is a personal God, but also that he is a finite being. God is greater than any other being, yet even he is limited in some significant respects. God could be greater than he is now.

If a person is limited in what he can know or do, those limitations often are imposed by the existence of *other* people. For example, I'm limited in how quickly I can drive to work because there are other drivers on the roads. The amount of money I can earn is limited by the willingness and ability of other people to pay for my services, whether some people are offering similar services, and so on. Other people are the reason I can't win every eBay auction at a bargain price. In almost every area of life, I'm limited by the existence of others.

This observation has implications for Finite Theism. We have seen that some think there's a finite personal God, subject to many limitations. One plausible explanation for those limitations is simply that *God isn't alone*. God has competition, so to speak, from other divine beings. He has a peer group. The deity we call "God" isn't the *only* God.

This suggests that Finite Theists can be divided into two camps: those who think that there is only *one* finite deity and those who think that there are actually *multiple* finite deities. Some of these deities may be nicer, smarter, or stronger than others, but they're all divine beings. There's no *uniquely* divine being.

So, in which of these two camps do you pitch your tent?

Is there only one God? Is God a *uniquely* divine being?

**If you answered yes to the Uniqueness Question, go to page 63.**
**If you answered no to the Uniqueness Question, go to page 89.**

# The Communication Question

> HAS GOD COMMUNICATED WITH HUMANS?

Let's take stock. Based on your answers so far, we know you believe that there is one God who created and sustains the universe and who is both a *personal* being and a *perfect* being.

This means that you hold to a basically Monotheist ("one God") worldview. The three major Abrahamic religions—Christianity, Islam, and Judaism—all reflect a Monotheist worldview, although there are very significant differences between them, as we'll soon see.

At this point, we need to ask some further questions to narrow down your worldview.

You've indicated that, in your view, God is a *personal* being. One of the most distinctive characteristics of a person is the ability to *communicate*. People communicate with other people, and they do so in various ways: sometimes audibly, sometimes in writing, sometimes with gestures or other signs.

If God is indeed a personal being, this raises some obvious and highly significant questions: Does *God* communicate? *Has* God communicated?

If God is perfect in knowledge and power, it follows that he must have the *ability* to communicate with us, even if the way he communicates is somewhat different from the way we humans normally communicate.

So the question being asked at this point isn't whether God *can* communicate. Surely God can do so if he wants to. Rather, the question is whether God *has* communicated—at least with *some* humans, at some time or other. What do you think?

**If you answered yes to the Communication Question, go to page 35.**
**If you answered no to the Communication Question, go to page 61.**

# The Openness Question

> HAS GOD COMMUNICATED OPENLY TO HUMANS?

You answered yes to the Communication Question: God *has* communicated with humans. But now we need to probe a little deeper regarding *how* God has communicated.

The idea that God has communicated with humans—the technical term is "divine revelation"—is common in Theist worldviews. After all, that's very much what we'd *expect* if God were a personal Supreme Being who was perfect in goodness, wisdom, and power. Moreover, this divine revelation is usually understood to be a *public* revelation: God has spoken to humans openly and collectively (e.g., through prophets and inspired scriptures) rather than secretly and individually.

It may be that not every human being has immediate access to this public divine revelation, just as not every human being has immediate access to the works of Shakespeare, but *in principle* all people could hear or read God's communication for themselves. It's not a secret, hidden, private revelation; it's available in principle to anyone and everyone.

Nevertheless, a Theist might take a different view on this key issue. You might think that God has communicated with humans, but that he has always done so *privately* and *individually*, rather like a tutor giving private lessons to each of his students. On this view, God said privately to Jack what Jack needed to hear, he said privately to Jill what Jill needed to hear, and so on down the line.

So, which do you think is the case? Has God communicated openly and collectively to humans (as opposed to communicating only privately and individually)?

**If you answered yes to the Openness Question, go to page 36.**
**If you answered no to the Openness Question, go to page 73.**

# The Resurrection Question

> DID JESUS OF NAZARETH RISE FROM THE DEAD?

Now we're getting down into the details. Your answers to the questions so far have revealed that you hold a Classical Theist worldview with a public revelation. You believe there is a personal God who is perfect in every way, who created the universe, and who has communicated openly with the humans he created.

You might think that the question on this page is a little premature, perhaps even prejudicial. Why are we talking about Jesus all of a sudden? Isn't that biased against religions such as Judaism that don't center on Jesus?

Not at all. At this point, we're only asking a question: a key question that will help to further narrow the field of worldviews you might hold. Finding out what a Theist believes about Jesus is arguably the most effective way to identify what worldview he or she has, because every major Theist worldview takes a distinctive position on who Jesus really was, what he did, and what happened to him.

One of the distinctive claims of *Christian* Theism is that Jesus of Nazareth, the man whose life is described in the four biblical Gospels, died by crucifixion but was miraculously raised to life again only a few days later. Christianity teaches that this was a literal, physical, bodily resurrection: Jesus returned from the dead with the same body that was nailed to the cross.[1] It wasn't merely a metaphorical or "spiritual" resurrection, as if the Gospels were saying, "The spirit of Jesus lived on in the hearts of his disciples!"

Theists who aren't Christians usually deny the resurrection of Jesus. So this is a crucial dividing issue. On which side do *you* fall? Did Jesus of Nazareth rise from the dead?

**If you answered yes to the Resurrection Question, go to page 39.**
**If you answered no to the Resurrection Question, go to page 51.**

# The Muhammad Question

> WAS MUHAMMAD A TRUE PROPHET OF GOD?

Your answers so far tell us that you're a Theist, and a fairly traditional one, but you're not a *Christian* Theist. Since you believe God has communicated to humans in a public way, you're most likely an adherent of one of the other major monotheistic faiths—Islam or Judaism.

One possibility is that you're a Muslim, a follower of the religion of Islam. The most direct way to determine whether someone is a Muslim is to ask about his view of Muhammad. Muslims believe that Muhammad (AD 570–632) was a true prophet of God, whereas non-Muslims reject that strong claim (even if they think Muhammad was a good person or a religious reformer worthy of respect).

What exactly do we mean by "a true prophet of God"? It doesn't necessarily refer to a person who can predict the future, although a prophet might do that. Rather, a true prophet of God is someone who can be considered a genuine spokesperson for God, by God's own appointment. The prophet is merely a messenger; the message he delivers is nothing less than a revelation from God. His prophetic teaching therefore has all the authority of God.

Muslims believe that Muhammad was the last (and perhaps the greatest) of God's prophets and that his message from God is recorded in the Qur'an, the most holy book of Islam.

What do *you* believe about Muhammad? Was he a true prophet of God?

**If you answered yes to the Muhammad Question, go to page 65.**
**If you answered no to the Muhammad Question, go to page 38.**

# The Moses Question

> WAS MOSES A TRUE PROPHET OF GOD?

With our last couple of questions, we've been narrowing your options among traditional Theist worldviews. Since you don't believe that Jesus of Nazareth rose from the dead, as the New Testament clearly teaches, you can't be a *Christian* Theist. And since you don't believe that Muhammad was a true prophet, you're not an *Islamic* Theist. So we've eliminated two out of the three major Abrahamic religions.

The third of these religions is Judaism, of course. In common with Christianity and Islam, Judaism holds Abraham in high regard. But unlike Christianity and Islam, Judaism denies that Jesus of Nazareth was a true prophet of God. (Islam teaches that Jesus was a true prophet, but not the Son of God, as Christians claim.)

For Christians, Jesus is undoubtedly the greatest of the prophets (and much more besides). For Muslims, Muhammad is the greatest of the prophets. But whom do Jews consider to be the greatest prophet?

The obvious candidate is Moses, whom many Jews refer to as "the Father of the Prophets." According to Jewish tradition, Moses was chosen by God to lead the Israelites, the ancient Jewish people, out of slavery in Egypt and into the Promised Land. God spoke to the Israelites through Moses, who received the Ten Commandments on Mount Sinai and wrote the Torah (the first five books of the Hebrew Bible) under divine instruction.

One of the defining claims of Judaism, then, is that Moses was a true prophet of God. Do you agree?

**If you answered yes to the Moses Question, go to page 67.**
**If you answered no to the Moses Question, go to page 77.**

# The Divinity Question

> WAS JESUS OF NAZARETH DIVINE?

You might think that anyone who believes that Jesus rose from the dead must be a Christian. That person must hold a Christian Theist worldview—end of story. So why more questions?

Surprising as it may seem, there are a few people who think that Jesus may well have returned from the dead but who don't consider themselves Christians because they disagree with other central teachings of Christianity. To put it in logical terms, the belief that Jesus rose from the dead is *necessary* for a Christian worldview, but it isn't *sufficient*. Christianity is much more than the claim that Jesus of Nazareth rose from the dead.

One of the other central teachings of Christianity that distinguishes it from alternative worldviews is the claim that Jesus was more than a mere human being. The first Christians didn't merely admire Jesus. They *worshiped* him. As one early Roman observer wrote, those Christians sang hymns "to Christ as to a god."[2] In fact, the New Testament portrays Jesus as *divine*. It claims that he existed as a divine person even before he was conceived in his mother's womb and that he was involved in the creation of the universe.[3]

Needless to say, these are extremely bold claims! It's true that Christians have disagreed over some of the details of what exactly it means to say that Jesus is divine. But all the major Christian traditions, from the earliest centuries, have firmly held that Jesus is no less than God incarnate: God living among us in human form.

But what do *you* think? Was Jesus of Nazareth really divine?

**If you answered yes to the Divinity Question, go to page 40.**
**If you answered no to the Divinity Question, go to page 95.**

# The Salvation Question

> DO GOOD PEOPLE GO TO HEAVEN AND BAD PEOPLE TO HELL?

Your answers so far are in line with a Christian worldview. You believe in a personal God who created the universe and who has communicated openly with human beings. You also believe that Jesus of Nazareth was no ordinary man: he was the divine Son of God who rose from the dead. It's highly unlikely you would hold these beliefs unless you also believed that the Bible (or at least the New Testament) is a divine revelation, since the Bible is the basis for these distinctive Christian teachings.

There is, however, one more question to ask before we can precisely identify your worldview: a question about *salvation*. Think back to the Goodness Question: you agreed that some things are objectively good or bad. This fits perfectly with a Christian worldview, in which God is the ultimate standard of goodness. Good people are those who truly love God, the ultimate good, and love their fellow humans, who are made in the image of God.[4] Conversely, bad people are those who fall short of loving God and their fellow humans as they should.

In keeping with the teachings of Jesus, Christians also believe in heaven and hell. The Bible refers to heaven as "eternal life": never-ending bliss in the presence of God. The dire alternative is hell, which might well be described as "eternal death": permanent separation from God and everything that is good.

But what determines your final destination? One very common view is simply this: good people go to heaven and bad people go to hell. Do you agree? Is eternal life the reward for those of us who live a good enough life here and now?

**If you answered yes to the Salvation Question, go to page 83.**
**If you answered no to the Salvation Question, go to page 59.**

Part II

# CATEGORIES

# Atheist Worldviews

Atheism is simply the view that there is no God, no Supreme Being that deserves our worship and gives meaning and direction to the universe and human life. (Atheism shouldn't be confused with agnosticism, which is the view that there may or may not be a God, but we don't know or can't know either way.) Atheism has been a minority view in human history and remains so today, even in supposedly secular societies. Still, that fact alone doesn't mean that it's wrong. The real issue is whether Atheism makes better overall sense of the world than the alternatives.

It's often said that there is no Atheist *worldview*, because Atheism is only a negative claim ("There is no God") and because Atheists can have widely differing views on other important matters. Even so, we can say that there are Atheist *worldviews*—in other words, there are a number of worldviews that answer no to the God Question. The remaining questions will help us to differentiate between these Atheist worldviews.

Precisely because Atheist worldviews share the belief that there is no God, they share a troublesome problem. Earlier, you answered yes to the Goodness Question: you agreed that at least some things are *objectively* good or bad, not merely a matter of human tastes or preferences. If there is a God, this affirmative answer makes perfect sense. As the Supreme Being, God is the ultimate standard of goodness in the universe; God, we might say, is the ultimate good. Whatever conforms to God is good and praiseworthy. God is thus the ultimate basis for the distinction between good and evil.

Obviously this explanation isn't open to the Atheist. Indeed, one of the toughest challenges Atheist worldviews face is explaining how anything can be objectively good or bad if there's no God to serve as the ultimate standard of goodness. The same goes for objective meaning and purpose: if there's no God, then it seems that the universe can have no ultimate meaning, purpose, or direction. The universe just is what it is and does what it does; there's really no good or bad about it, objectively speaking.

CATEGORIES

For these very reasons, many Atheist thinkers bite the bullet and give up altogether the idea that anything is objectively good or bad, along with the idea that the universe has any ultimate significance. In other words, they argue that a consistent Atheist should also be a Nihilist (see page 75).

But since you answered yes to the Goodness Question, you must think these Atheists are mistaken. So where exactly does their reasoning go wrong? The challenge is to explain how Atheism can avoid being dragged into the black hole of Nihilism.

**To reconsider the God Question, go to page 25.**
**To reconsider the Religion Question, go to page 24.**
**To reconsider the Goodness Question, go to page 23.**
**Otherwise, continue to page 26.**

# Theist Worldviews

Theism, as I'm defining it here, is simply the belief that there is a God: there is at least one divine being. For our purposes, we will treat Theism as a fairly broad category, one that allows for various conceptions of God and even for the possibility that there are many gods. In other words, there are various Theist worldviews, and the differences between them turn out to be extremely significant. The remaining questions will help us to narrow down the field and to identify more precisely *which* Theist worldview you hold.

It's worth noting at this point that your answers to the previous questions fit very nicely with one another. For example, you answered yes to the Goodness Question: you believe that there is a real, objective distinction between good and evil. It's widely recognized that Theist worldviews can account for this distinction far more easily than Atheist worldviews. If there's a real, objective distinction between good and evil, then there must be an ultimate standard of goodness in the universe—and that ultimate standard is simply God.

Goodness, in the final analysis, is *godliness*: to be good is to be in conformity with God. As noted earlier, without God as the ultimate good, it's very hard to justify the claim that "good" and "bad" are anything above and beyond mere human tastes and preferences. So Theism has a distinct advantage over Atheism on this point.

Nevertheless, Theism faces challenges of its own. Arguably the greatest challenge that Theist worldviews face is the problem of evil. If there really is a God, why is there so much evil in the world? In fact, why is there evil *at all*? It's important to realize that Theists have addressed this problem in very different ways depending on their views of God. Exactly what you think God is like, and how you think God relates to the world, determines how—and how well—you're able to account for the existence of evil in the world.

The problem of evil is a formidable challenge for Theists, and they have penned thousands of books over the centuries as they have wrestled with the perplexing questions it raises. Even so, Theists often point out to their Atheist critics that they'd much rather face the lesser problem of accounting for evil than the greater problem of accounting for *both* good *and* evil! (For more on this point, pay a short visit to page 43—but don't forget to come back here!)

**To reconsider the God Question, go to page 25.**
**To reconsider the Religion Question, go to page 24.**
**To reconsider the Goodness Question, go to page 23.**
**Otherwise, continue to page 29.**

# Quasi-Theist Worldviews

Quasi-Theism, as I'm using the term, is the view that there is a God, but that deity isn't a personal being in any sense with which we're familiar. Perhaps God is more like "the Force" in the *Star Wars* movies, a transcendent supercomputer, or a divine ordering principle for the universe. Or perhaps God is *all* of reality, taken as a whole, whereas our universe is only one part of that reality.

Quasi-Theism marks a deviation from what's known as Classical Theism, which represents a more traditional religious view of God as the all-good, all-powerful, personal Creator of the universe.

Quasi-Theism certainly holds some important advantages over Atheism. For instance, it may be able to explain why an orderly physical universe exists: God brought the universe into existence and continues to sustain and direct it. Atheist worldviews can't offer any explanation like that because they deny the existence of any transcendent ordering cause of the universe. In the end, Atheists have to accept the existence of the orderly physical universe as a "brute fact" (which is really no explanation at all).

However, Quasi-Theism also faces some general difficulties and perplexities. In the first place, there are strong scientific reasons for thinking that our universe is designed to support intelligent, conscious life-forms like us. Scientists are discovering that many of the fundamental laws and physical constants of the universe appear to be "fine-tuned" to accommodate such life-forms. If the universe really does show the marks of design, it must have a Designer. There must be an intelligent mind behind it.

But could there be an intelligent mind that doesn't belong to a *person*? (Computers are intelligent in a certain sense, but don't forget that they first had to be designed by *people* like us!) In short, the only *original* intelligences we know about are *personal* beings. Since Quasi-Theism denies that God is a personal being, it doesn't offer the best explanation of the design of the universe.

Here's another difficulty for Quasi-Theism. God is typically considered to be *perfect*, a Supreme Being that is greater in every respect than any other being. But wouldn't it be greater to possess self-consciousness, intelligence, affections, and the power of free choice than to lack all those capacities?

If so, it follows that a *perfect* being cannot be less than a *personal* being. And that means Quasi-Theists should also deny that God is a perfect being—which only raises further questions. (If God isn't the standard of perfection, who or what *is*? Would a God who is neither personal nor perfect be worthy of our love and our worship?)

Despite these challenges, there are many religious believers in the world today (not to mention a fair number of non-religious thinkers) who hold to a Quasi-Theist worldview as a sort of middle ground between Atheism and Classical Theism.

**To reconsider the Personality Question, go to page 29.**
**To reconsider the God Question, go to page 25.**
**Otherwise, continue to page 30.**

# Finite Theist Worldviews

Finite Theism is the view that there is a God—a Supreme Being who is worthy of worship and gives meaning and direction to the universe—but God isn't a *perfect* being. At least, God isn't perfect in every respect. For example, God *could* be greater in goodness, greater in knowledge, or greater in power than he actually is now. Finite Theists sometimes claim that God is developing and maturing: he is becoming better and better, moving closer to perfection, but he isn't absolutely perfect yet (and may never be).

Another way to express this view is to say that God, like us, is a *finite* being rather than an infinite being (hence the term *Finite Theist*). God is no doubt a whole lot nicer, smarter, and stronger than the rest of us, but he still has significant limitations. (You may remember the classic line by Clint Eastwood's Dirty Harry character: "A man's got to know his limitations." If you have a Finite Theist worldview, you've got to know *God's* limitations, too.)

Finite Theists often say that their view of God helps to explain why our world is less than perfect: it is imperfect precisely because it's the product of a God who is imperfect. Still, it seems rather odd on the face of it to say that God isn't perfect. After all, if *God* isn't perfect, who or what *is*?

In fact, there seems to be a deep incoherence here. The very idea of imperfection implies a *standard* of perfection. If God is imperfect in some respects, presumably there must be some standard or measure of perfection compared to which God is falling short. But then that standard or measure of perfection, whatever it is, would seem to be greater and more ultimate than God. So why not call *that* thing "God" instead, If "God" is, by definition, the *Supreme* Being? If, on the other hand, there's no such ultimate standard or measure of perfection, what sense does it make to say that God is *imperfect*?

Finite Theism raises some other disconcerting questions. Here's just one: if God is limited in his knowledge or in his power, is he really in control of the universe? In other words, does God sometimes

CATEGORIES

experience nasty surprises and humiliating defeats like we do? If so, is God really worthy of our adoration and our worship? Is he worthy of our *trust*?

As the saying goes, "The bigger they come, the harder they fall." If God can fall, the worry is that we're all going to get flattened.

**To reconsider the Perfection Question, go to page 32.**
**To reconsider the Personality Question, go to page 29.**
**To reconsider the God Question, go to page 25.**
**Otherwise, continue to page 33.**

# Non-Christian Theist Worldviews

According to the New Testament, if Jesus wasn't raised from the dead, then he wasn't the Son of God, and the Christian faith is vain and futile.[5] In other words, if the resurrection of Jesus didn't really happen, then Christianity is flat-out false. So it's fair to say that anyone with a Theist worldview who denies or seriously doubts that Jesus rose from the dead has a *Non-Christian* Theist worldview.

However, Jesus remains one of the most significant challenges for anyone with a Non-Christian Theist worldview. Simply put, what do you *do* with Jesus?

It's hard to deny that Jesus of Nazareth was a real historical person (arguably the single most influential person in history), that he claimed to be the Son of God who had come to die a sacrificial death for the sins of his people, and that he predicted his resurrection from the dead.[6] So if Jesus wasn't who he claimed to be, was he a madman or a con man? Neither of those profiles fits him. The four Gospels present a consistent picture of a well-adjusted and pious man who was fully in control of himself and his destiny, a charismatic religious leader who was willing to lay down his life for the sake of others.

Many people who can't accept that Jesus was a fraudster or mentally unhinged prefer to say that he was simply a great moral teacher. But that's hard to square with everything that we know about him. What kind of great moral teacher would make the outrageous claims that Jesus made? Would someone who intended to be only a moral teacher claim to have descended from heaven, to be equal with God, to have the right to forgive the sins of complete strangers, or to have authority over the entire universe?[7]

Others are content to say that Jesus was entirely sincere in all these claims, but sincerely mistaken. Yet once again, on closer examination this suggestion seems pretty hard to swallow. It's not as though his claims were on a par with those of someone who believes he's discovered the secret of alchemy or the location of the ark of the covenant. Jesus's claims weren't merely eccentric; they were utterly fantastical. Could a good man in his right mind be sincerely mistaken about all the things Jesus claimed about himself?

Another view is that his claims have been misunderstood, that Jesus *really* meant that we're *all* divine in some sense, just as many Eastern religions teach. This would make Jesus a very poor teacher, however, since it implies that everyone in his day completely misunderstood what he was teaching!

A further difficulty for those who reject the traditional Christian view of Jesus concerns how one deals with the historical evidence for his resurrection. All four of the biblical Gospels present themselves as historical eyewitness accounts.[8] Historians agree that Jesus of Nazareth was a real person who was crucified by the Romans around the year AD 30. It's also widely accepted that his disciples were convinced they had *seen* Jesus alive again several days after his execution and burial; they even claimed to have talked and eaten with him.[9] In fact, the Christian church was founded on their eyewitness testimony that Jesus had risen from the dead in fulfillment of prophecies in the Old Testament and his own predictions.[10] His followers were willing to be mocked, persecuted, and even killed rather than renounce their claims. What did they stand to gain?

Anyone who holds to a Theist worldview ought to agree that an all-powerful God *could* have raised Jesus from the dead. But if that wasn't what really happened after Jesus's crucifixion, what exactly *did* happen? What *better* explanation for the historical evidence is there? The challenge for Non-Christian Theists is to come up with an account that makes better sense of what we know about Jesus of Nazareth and the origins of the Christian church than the traditional Christian account.

**To reconsider the Resurrection Question, go to page 36.
Otherwise, continue to page 37.**

# Part III

# WORLDVIEWS

# Worldview: Atheistic Dualism

Dualism is the view that reality falls into two basic categories: the *material* (or physical) and the *mental* (or experiential). Everything that exists is either material or mental, or some composite of the two. Dualism also holds that these categories are fundamentally distinct: you can't explain the mental in purely material terms or vice versa. There are material things, such as your brain and its neurological processes, and there are also mental things, such as your mind and its rational thoughts. For the Dualist, your mind is necessarily distinct from your brain, although the two (somehow) interact. Your brain has features (such as being gray and squishy) that your mind doesn't have. Your mind has features (such as the capacity to form ideas and intentions) that your brain doesn't have.

Since you earlier answered no to the God Question, the Dualist worldview we're considering now is Atheistic Dualism. On this view, there is no ultimate mind behind the universe. There are only finite minds, like yours and mine, interacting with a finite material universe via our bodies.

Dualism has the virtue of not denying what seems quite obvious to most people: we really do have both minds and bodies. Nevertheless, Atheistic Dualism faces great difficulties answering some fundamental questions, including: Where did mind and matter come from in the first place? Did mind spring forth from pure matter at some point in time? But how could matter alone produce something so radically different from it?

Our experience of the world tells us that intelligence doesn't come out of nowhere. You don't get intelligence for free or by accident. For example, a computer is a purely physical thing that exhibits a kind of intelligence, but only because its material parts have been arranged and directed by a preexisting intelligence.

So how could intelligent minds arise out of pure mindless matter without the direction of a preexisting intelligence? Atheistic Dualism, which denies that human life was designed or planned by any higher intelligence, asks us to believe that you *can* get intelligence for free and by sheer accident—at least if you wait long enough!

Even if these difficulties can be overcome, Atheistic Dualism faces further objections. Here's just one to think about. You're probably familiar with the phrase "mind over matter." Could mind ever be *over* matter in an Atheistic Dualist worldview? Could minds exercise independent control over the material realm?

The standard Atheist view is that all life on Earth is the result of billions of years of gradual evolution from mindless, single-celled organisms via undirected natural processes. But if our minds are the product of purely material processes, it seems to follow that our mental lives are completely conditioned by the underlying physical processes of our brains. Just as the course of a stream running down a mountainside is determined entirely by material laws and processes, so our ideas and decisions are determined entirely by material laws and processes. Given this view of human origins, it's very hard to see how our minds could *transcend* the mindless physical laws and processes that gave birth to them.

But if that is the case, what room does Atheistic Dualism leave for freedom of thought or freedom of choice? What room does it leave for a book like this one?

You've reached the end of the trail. However:

**To reconsider the Mind Question, go to page 28.**
**To reconsider the Matter Question, go to page 27.**
**To reconsider the Unity Question, go to page 26.**
**To reconsider the God Question, go to page 25.**

# Worldview: Atheistic Idealism

Idealism is the philosophical term for the view that everything is ultimately *mental* in nature. It holds that nothing exists apart from minds and the ideas within those minds (hence *idealism*). Idealists believe that what we call material things, such as trees and tables, aren't *really* objects that exist independently of our minds and our sensory experiences, despite what many people assume. According to the Idealist, trees and tables are only ideas in minds. A tree is really just a *tree idea* or a *tree experience*. A table is really just a *table idea* or a *table experience*. If there were no minds with ideas and experiences, there would be no trees, tables, or anything else. One influential Idealist, George Berkeley, put it this way: "To be is to be perceived."[11] In other words, nothing exists unless it is perceived by a mind.

An Idealist doesn't have to be an Atheist. Berkeley, for example, was a *Theistic* Idealist. He argued that there had to be a divine mind in addition to our human minds. But since you answered no to the God Question, you must be an Atheistic Idealist.

Atheistic Idealism isn't nearly as popular today as Materialism (see page 69), although many argue that it's far more reasonable than Materialism precisely because it doesn't ultimately deny the reality of our mental lives—including our reasoning! If reason is a feature of minds, only a worldview that affirms the reality of minds can be considered reasonable. So at least Atheistic Idealism has that advantage over Materialism.

Nevertheless, Atheistic Idealism faces some formidable difficulties. First, it seems very counterintuitive. Isn't it a matter of common sense that trees and tables are real material objects that exist independently of our minds? If we can't trust our common sense on that basic issue, how could we trust it on anything else?

What's more, Atheistic Idealism seems to have the extraordinary implication that if every mind in the universe were destroyed, then the universe itself would cease to exist. It also implies that there has always existed *at least one mind*, because Idealism says that nothing exists independently of minds. So even at the big bang, there must have been one or more minds. But that's quite at odds with the theory of evolution, which most Atheists want to accept. According to the theory of evolution, minds are the product of prior material processes. They're latecomers in the universe!

Here's another tricky question for the Atheistic Idealist. Each of us has vivid and orderly experiences of a unified material world. If those experiences aren't caused by real material objects, what *are* they caused by? Idealism says they ultimately must be caused by minds rather than material things. But *which* minds?

One possible answer is *other* human minds. But could all of your unique and complex experiences of the world really be caused by the minds of other human beings? That seems rather hard to swallow, not to mention quite disconcerting!

Another answer is *your* mind. It's reasonable to think that *some* of your experiences and ideas are caused by your own mind (dreams, for example). Perhaps, then, *all* of your experiences and ideas are caused by your own mind. But if that's the case, what need is there for any other mind to explain your experiences of the world? As more than a few philosophers have noted, Atheistic Idealism is in danger of sliding into solipsism, the view that your own mind is the only mind that really exists. But in that case, who really wrote this book?

One way out of this problem is to say that there is one absolute mind that causes every other mind to have orderly, coordinated experiences of a unified reality. But wouldn't that be tantamount to admitting there is a God after all?

You've reached the end of the trail. However:

**To reconsider the Mind Question, go to page 28.**
**To reconsider the Matter Question, go to page 27.**
**To reconsider the Unity Question, go to page 26.**
**To reconsider the God Question, go to page 25.**

# Worldview: Christianity

Christianity is the largest religion in the world today, claiming around one-third of the world population. Christianity, of course, is centered on Jesus Christ, whom Christians consider to be not merely a great prophet and spiritual teacher, but the divine Son of God and the Savior of the world.[12]

According to the Christian worldview, there is a personal God who is perfect in goodness, knowledge, and power. God created the entire universe out of nothing and continually sustains it.[13] We humans were uniquely created in his image to live in personal love relationships with him and with our fellow humans.[14] It therefore follows that there are objective moral standards for human life: God's good and wise commandments, which can be summarized in terms of loving him and loving our neighbors.[15]

Tragically, however, we humans rebelled against our Creator and flouted his perfect moral laws. By doing so, we spoiled God's creation, corrupted ourselves, and placed ourselves under his righteous judgment.[16] We are all rebels at heart and deserve only condemnation, yet out of his great love and mercy God sent a Savior, in the person of his divine Son, Jesus Christ, to restore us and reconcile us to God. Jesus accomplished this by his sacrificial death on the cross for our sins and his resurrection from the dead.[17] God has revealed this salvation plan through his prophets, his apostles, and (of course) Jesus himself.[18] These revelations are recorded in the Bible, which consists of the Old and New Testaments.

The greatest challenge for the Christian worldview is undoubtedly the problem of evil. If God is perfect and created everything good, why is there evil in the world—and so much of it? The Bible suggests a number of reasons why God would allow evil for a greater good purpose, but it doesn't answer every question. In the end, one has to decide whether the Christian worldview, when compared with other worldviews, provides the best *overall* account of the fundamental distinction between good and evil, and of our experience of good and evil in the world.

All things considered, the Christian worldview has a lot going for it. It's a philosophically rich and existentially satisfying worldview that can readily account for many of the basic features of the universe and human life that we take for granted. What's more, it has one truly extraordinary asset: Jesus of Nazareth, who is arguably the most captivating, provocative, and influential person in human history, whatever view you take of him.

Ironically, however, many people find Christianity's greatest asset to be its greatest problem as well. Born in obscurity and poverty, Jesus claimed to be "lowly in heart" and a servant of all—yet he also claimed to be equal with God and received worship from his disciples.[19] He demanded moral perfection from his followers and required them to sacrifice everything for his sake—yet he also promised them the world.[20] His entrance requirements for heaven were impossibly high—yet he welcomed the most immoral of people into the kingdom of God.[21] He rejected political office and had no permanent home—yet he also claimed to have divine authority over the entire universe.[22] He displayed divine powers, even the power to overcome death—yet he willingly submitted himself to one of the most painful and shameful deaths imaginable.[23] He claimed he hadn't come to judge the world—yet he also declared that he would return at the end of history and do precisely that.[24]

What exactly do you do with someone like that? You can't ignore him. You have to find *some* place for him in your worldview. But if you don't put Jesus right at the center, where else could he go?

You've reached the end of the trail. However:

**To reconsider the Salvation Question, go to page 40.**
**To reconsider the Divinity Question, go to page 39.**
**To reconsider the Resurrection Question, go to page 36.**

# Worldview: Deism

Deism is the view that there is a God, but he remains "at a distance" and doesn't intervene at all in the natural workings of the universe. For the Deist, the universe was created by God, but it now operates entirely according to natural principles, such as the laws of physics, and there are no supernatural events such as miracles or divine revelation (e.g., God communicating with us through prophecies or visions). Deists sometimes use this analogy: God is like a watchmaker who designs and constructs a watch, but after winding it up, he lets it run on its own, with no further supervision or intervention.

Self-described Deists often consider themselves religious—they believe in a Creator God, after all—but they tend not to associate closely with any of the major world religions, simply because belief in supernatural intervention and divine revelation is central to those religions. On the other hand, it's fair to say that many people in the West who identify themselves as Christians or Jews have worldviews closer to Deism. Deists typically believe that there are objective moral laws, but they say that these laws are derived from nature or human experience rather than divine revelation (such as the Bible).

Some Deists have held that God isn't a personal being. (If you agree with them, go back and review your answer to the Personality Question, page 29!) However, if the Creator of the universe isn't personal, that raises some difficult questions (for more on this point, see page 47). Deists who believe that God is a personal being are in a stronger position, but even so, they face a very perplexing scenario: Why would a personal Supreme Being create intelligent personal beings with the capacity for verbal communication and then *never* speak to them? Not even a quick "Hello"?

Here's an analogy to drive the point home. Imagine that a brilliant and benevolent scientist creates an intelligent, humanlike robot that has the capacity for meaningful conversation with him (think Data from *Star Trek: The Next Generation* or Sonny from the movie *I, Robot*). This scientist, however, never actually converses with his creation.

Wouldn't that be very odd and surprising? Why would a scientist create a robot with that capacity but never give the robot an opportunity to exercise that capacity? In the same way, it would be very odd and surprising for God to create us with the capacity for verbal communication but never say a single word to us!

This oddity of Deism is compounded by the problem of evil. Clearly we've made a mess of the world God created. We've dug holes for ourselves that we struggle to escape. There is a great deal of suffering in the world, much of it caused by us and much of it beyond our control. If God is truly all-good, all-wise, and all-powerful, as Deists believe, wouldn't we expect him to step in and sort things out? Wouldn't we expect God at least to offer a helping hand or a few words of advice?

Deism was very popular among the intellectuals of the eighteenth and nineteenth centuries, but over time it gave way to full-blown Atheism, and it's not too difficult to see why. Deism is arguably just a halfway house on the road from Theism to Atheism. For all practical purposes, a deity who is distant and silent might as well not exist at all. A mute God might as well be a dead God.

You've reached the end of the trail. However:

**To reconsider the Communication Question, go to page 34.**
**To reconsider the Perfection Question, go to page 32.**
**To reconsider the Personality Question, go to page 29.**

# Worldview: Finite Godism

Finite Godism is the view that there is a personal God who created and directs the world, but he is a *finite* being and is limited in significant ways by factors external to him. According to this worldview, God isn't *absolutely perfect*—at least, not in every respect. Those who hold to Finite Godism usually insist that God is perfect in goodness—his thoughts and actions are always morally pure—but his knowledge and power are limited. They argue that the existence of an orderly natural universe can be explained only by the presence of a transcendent supernatural Creator, but if God is limited in what he knows about the future and what he can do in the present, that helps to explain why there is evil in the universe he created. In short, the universe exists only because God exists, but the universe is less than perfect because God is less than perfect.

We've already considered some of the basic problems faced by Finite Theist worldviews (see page 49), but more can be said. In the first place, Finite Godism may be arbitrary in the way it ascribes limitations to God. For example, why should we think that God is limited in power rather than limited in goodness? Wouldn't an *all-powerful-but-partly-evil* God explain the presence of evil in our universe just as well as an *all-good-but-partly-weak* God?

In any case, it's far from obvious that Finite Godism offers a satisfying answer to the problem of evil. Even if God isn't *infinitely* powerful, surely he's still more powerful than anything else. (After all, he created the universe!) But in that case, couldn't God have stopped Adolf Hitler, Joseph Stalin, and Pol Pot? Couldn't he have prevented the 9/11 terrorist attacks? Couldn't he have stopped the South Asian tsunami in 2004 and Hurricane Katrina in 2005? Is God's power so limited that he can't even save a child from being hit by a car?

On closer inspection, then, Finite Godism doesn't really solve the one theological problem it promises to solve. Either God has sufficient knowledge and power to prevent all these evils or he simply isn't worthy of the title "God." It makes little sense to think that God is smart

WORLDVIEWS

and powerful enough to *create* this universe but not smart and powerful enough to *keep it under control* once it is created. A finite God is arguably no God at all, which suggests that the real choice is between an infinite God and no God.

As you're no doubt aware, the "no God" option has its own problems (for more on this point, see page 43). But if you want to hold on to a Theist worldview, you may find it more coherent and satisfying to say this: God is perfect in *every* respect, and he ultimately has good and wise reasons for permitting all the evils in the world, even if we, with our finite minds, aren't able to figure out all of those reasons.

You've reached the end of the trail. However:

**To reconsider the Uniqueness Question, go to page 33.**
**To reconsider the Perfection Question, go to page 32.**
**To reconsider the Personality Question, go to page 29.**

# Worldview: Islam

Islam is one of the three major Abrahamic religions, and its adherents account for about one-fifth of the world's population. Islam holds to a strict Monotheist ("one God") worldview. It teaches that there is a transcendent God, Allah, who created the universe and sustains it. Islam places great emphasis on the idea of law: the natural world is governed by divine law, and so are human beings. Our highest goal is to know the laws of Allah and to submit ourselves completely to him by observing those laws. (The word *Islam* literally means "submission" or "surrender.")

Allah has revealed his laws to humans by speaking through various prophets or messengers, such as Abraham, Moses, David, Jesus, and Muhammad. Islam recognizes various holy books, including the Law of Moses (the Torah), the Psalms of David, and the Gospel of Jesus.[25] However, the Qur'an, which, according to Muslim tradition, was dictated by an angel to Muhammad, is considered to be the last and greatest of the holy books. The Qur'an and the Hadith (traditions about the life and sayings of the prophet Muhammad) serve as the primary sources for Islamic law.

One of the central teachings of Islam is that there will be a final day of judgment. On that day, all of our words and deeds will be weighed in the balance of divine justice. Those who have believed in Allah and lived good enough lives will be rewarded with pleasures in paradise, while the rest will be punished with torments in hell.[26]

Muslims don't think that you have to live an absolutely perfect life to enter paradise. They insist that Allah is compassionate and merciful, and can forgive the sins of those who believe in him and love him (though no one should ever *presume* upon Allah's forgiveness). However, there seems to be a tension within Islam between the justice and the mercy of Allah. If justice is to be satisfied, every violation of the law should receive its just penalty. Therefore, an absolutely perfect judge would ensure that no crime goes unpunished. According to Islam, however, Allah simply chooses to overlook some people's sins.

How, then, can he be an absolutely perfect judge? Does Allah consistently uphold his own just laws? The problem for Islam is that, unlike Christianity, it has no doctrine of atonement that could explain how God could forgive human sins without violating his own principles of justice.

Another difficulty for Islam is the fact that there are many contradictions between its holy books. For example, all four Gospel accounts state that Jesus claimed to be the Son of God and was killed by crucifixion, whereas the Qur'an denies both.[27] Muslims typically deal with these conflicts by arguing that the earlier holy books, although given by Allah, have been lost or corrupted. Only the last book, the Qur'an, is pure and uncorrupted.

This may solve the initial problem, but it introduces several new difficulties. In the first place, the Qur'an itself states that Allah will preserve his words from corruption.[28] But if that's true, how could those other holy books have become corrupted? Moreover, if Allah didn't prevent those earlier books from becoming badly corrupted, how can Muslims be confident today that the Qur'an hasn't *also* become corrupted? Why should we trust the Qur'an any more than those other books?

Interestingly, the Qur'an seems to assume that the holy books of the Jews and the Christians were trustworthy sources in Muhammad's day—trustworthy enough to confirm the prophet's message.[29] Yet we have ancient manuscripts of those books that have been dated well before Muhammad's birth, and they haven't changed since then.[30] If these books were trustworthy then and are still trustworthy today, but they contradict the teachings of the Qur'an, where does that leave the credibility of the Qur'an as a divine revelation?

You've reached the end of the trail. However:

**To reconsider the Muhammad Question, go to page 37.**
**To reconsider the Resurrection Question, go to page 36.**

# Worldview: Judaism

Judaism, the Jewish religion, has a long and distinguished pedigree. It traces its historical roots to the patriarch Abraham and bases its teachings on the Tanach (the Hebrew Bible, which Christians refer to as the Old Testament). Judaism clearly represents a Theist worldview, so it doesn't suffer from many of the problems faced by non-Theist worldviews. But there's much more to Judaism than its theology. In fact, modern Judaism places far more emphasis on how a person *lives* (observing the ancient Jewish traditions) than on what he or she *believes*.

At the very heart of Jewish practice is observance of the Torah: the law of God given to the Israelites at Mount Sinai through the prophet Moses. But equally important to Judaism is the Talmud, a lengthy collection of the opinions of thousands of Jewish rabbis (teachers of the law) on how to interpret and apply the Torah in everyday life.

One major challenge faced by Judaism can be stated in a single word: *Christianity*. Jesus of Nazareth was a first-century Jew who claimed to be the Messiah (literally "the Anointed One") promised by God to the Jewish people in the Hebrew Bible.[31] Only weeks after Jesus was crucified by the Romans in Jerusalem at the instigation of the Jewish leaders, his disciples began to preach that he had been raised from the dead.[32] They claimed to have seen Jesus alive again. He had even talked and eaten with them on several occasions. And they stuck to their story even in the face of persecution and death.

Following Jesus's example, his disciples argued that he was the fulfillment of all the prophecies about the Messiah in the Old Testament.[33] They made a good point: the Hebrew Bible does indeed contain many messianic prophecies that just beg to be fulfilled.[34] What's more, the prophecies seem to fit the circumstances of Jesus's life and death quite strikingly. If this remarkable Jesus of Nazareth wasn't the promised Messiah, who on earth could be? No other serious contender has appeared in the two thousand years since Jesus staked his claim.

The followers of Jesus posed another serious problem for Judaism. As I mentioned above, the requirement to observe the Torah lies at the very heart of Judaism.³⁵ But the Torah also teaches that anyone who fails to keep the law of God is under the curse of God.³⁶ But which of us could come anywhere close to keeping God's law perfectly so as to avoid that divine curse?

Christianity offers a striking solution to the problem posed by the Torah: Jesus, the perfect Son of God, bore the curse when he suffered and died on the cross—not on his own behalf (since he kept God's law at every point) but on behalf of his people.³⁷

Judaism rejects the messianic claims of Jesus and thus rejects the solution that Christianity offers. So what solution does Judaism offer for those who fail to keep the law of God?

Does it offer anything more substantial than "Try harder"?

You've reached the end of the trail. However:

**To reconsider the Moses Question, go to page 38.**
**To reconsider the Muhammad Question, go to page 37.**
**To reconsider the Resurrection Question, go to page 36.**

# Worldview: Materialism

Materialism is the view that everything is ultimately material in nature. At the most fundamental level, everything that exists consists of nothing but matter and energy. Everything is governed by the basic laws of physics and, in principle, can be completely explained in terms of those physical laws. Every object is a purely physical object. Every event that occurs has a purely physical cause (if it has any cause at all). In short, the universe is just a collection of clumps of matter following the laws of physics.

Materialists reject the idea that there are immaterial or spiritual entities, such as souls, angels, or God. For that reason, they deny that there is life after death. ("After you die, you rot," as more than one Materialist has said.) Materialism is the most widespread Atheist worldview in our day, mainly because of the extent to which modern science has come to dominate our view of the universe and ourselves. Science has been able to explain so much about the world that some people expect it will eventually explain *everything*. But science ultimately explains things in terms of matter and physical laws, so if science can explain *everything*, it follows that everything must be material in nature and governed by the laws of physics.

Many people find Materialism attractive because it places great emphasis on such scientific explanations. Its view of the basic constituents of the universe is relatively clear and uncluttered: only matter and energy exist.[38] Nevertheless, its advocates often don't recognize that it faces a number of formidable difficulties and challenges that make it hard to defend rationally.

For example, Materialism has great difficulty accounting for our mental lives and our conscious experience of the world. If you're a consistent Materialist, you ought to conclude either that you are literally mindless (which isn't a very appealing conclusion) or that minds and consciousness can be explained in entirely material terms (which no Materialist has been able to do). Minds, ideas, thoughts, and sensations are so very different from physical things that it's hard to see how they could be explained in purely physical terms. Physical things have physical features, such as size, shape, speed, and mass—but minds and ideas don't have those features. (What size is your mind? How much does it weigh?)

In contrast, ideas in our minds can be meaningful and true. But it makes no sense to ask what clumps of matter "mean" or whether they are "true"—unless those clumps of matter have been arranged in a meaningful way by a *mind* (for example, pebbles on a beach arranged to spell out "I love you").

There is a further difficulty for Materialism. Recall your earlier answer to the Goodness Question: you agreed that some things really are objectively good or bad. However, many philosophers have raised this question: If Materialism is true, what basis is there for claiming that anything in the universe is *objectively* good or bad, right or wrong? In a godless, mindless, purposeless material universe, on what basis could one clump of matter be ultimately considered any better or worse than any other clump of matter?

Clumps of matter as such aren't good or bad, right or wrong. They just are what they are and do what they do, following the laws of physics. So if human beings are ultimately just clumps of matter alongside all the other clumps of matter, what basis is there for making meaningful moral judgments about how human beings behave? In the Materialist worldview, the only real laws are the laws of physics. But the laws of physics only tell us how clumps of matter *do* behave. They tell us nothing at all about how clumps of matter *ought* to behave, in any meaningful moral sense.

You've reached the end of the trail. However:

**To reconsider the Matter Question, go to page 27.**
**To reconsider the Unity Question, go to page 26.**
**To reconsider the God Question, go to page 25.**

# Worldview: Monism

Monism (from the Greek word *monos*, meaning "single" or "alone") is the view that everything is ultimately one. Nothing that exists is really distinct from anything else that exists—which is just to say that, in the final analysis, only one thing exists. And that one thing—call it "the universe," "reality," "the One," or whatever you like—cannot be divided or decomposed into more fundamental parts or constituents. If it could, then reality would not be *ultimately* one. It would be ultimately *many*.

So the Monist has to say that the apparent diversity we experience in the world is an illusion. The distinctions we make between things are only in our minds, because if those things were *really* distinct from one another, there would be more than one thing in existence.

Monism is a very radical philosophy. It has generally proven more popular in Eastern philosophies and religions than in Western ones. While it has enjoyed some sophisticated defenders over the course of history, it faces some quite formidable objections.

In the first place, Monism is highly counterintuitive and flies in the face of our immediate sense experience. It asks us to disregard as illusory one of the most basic features of the world as it appears to us. It implies that our experiences of the world are thoroughly unreliable. After all, those experiences present us with a plurality of things: people, cats, dogs, trees, cars, doughnuts, cell phones, and the like. For the Monist, all these diverse things are either ultimately *identical* or ultimately *unreal*. Neither of these options is easy to swallow or to defend.

What's more, it's tough to live as a consistent Monist. Our everyday thoughts and decisions presuppose real distinctions between things: between your body and my body, between your spouse and my spouse, between your car and my car, between your credit card and my credit card, and so on.

And what goes for physical things such as our bodies must go for non-physical things such as our minds, as well. If Monism is true, your mind must be ultimately identical to my mind; your thoughts must be ultimately identical to my thoughts. But in that case, how could we disagree about anything? For example, how could we have different thoughts about whether or not Monism is true?

Here's one final question to ponder: Was your answer to the Unity Question consistent with your answers to all the earlier questions? Recall that you answered yes to the Truth Question, yes to the Knowledge Question, and yes to the Goodness Question. Those answers indicate that you believe in distinctions between truth and falsity, between knowledge and ignorance, and between goodness and badness.

Can a consistent Monist accept that those distinctions are real?

You've reached the end of the trail. However:

**To reconsider the Unity Question, go to page 26.**
**To reconsider the God Question, go to page 25.**

# Worldview: Mysticism

Mysticism (from the Greek word *mustikos*, meaning "secret") is perhaps the best label for a worldview that affirms the existence of God but rejects the idea that God has communicated with humans primarily through an *open* and *public* revelation, such as divinely inspired scriptures (as the Bible and the Qur'an claim to be). According to this view, God always speaks to people *privately* and *individually*. Strictly speaking, only I can really know what God says to me and only you can really know what God says to you. Moreover, what God says to you may well be very different from what God says to me.

Some who hold this view may accept that God speaks through ancient scriptures, such as the Bible, but they usually want to insist that the highest and most important knowledge of God comes through a direct personal experience of him. They may also want to say that God speaks through these scriptures in different ways to different people; with the same text, God can communicate one thing to Jack and quite another thing to Jill. What this means in practice is that while the actual *words* of the scriptures may be available to all, what God chooses to *communicate* through those words is always private and individual.

This worldview is appealing to some because it implies that God gives each of us direct, individual attention, rather like a personal physician or therapist. And there's certainly no shortage of people who claim to have received direct, private revelations from God!

Nevertheless, we have to consider how likely it is that God communicates only, or even primarily, in this fashion. If God wished to address human beings as a group, as an entire race, wouldn't an open and public revelation be much more fitting and practical? (By way of comparison, think of the public addresses given to an entire nation by the leader of that nation.) If all of us have the same basic needs and face the same basic challenges in life, surely it would make the most sense for God to speak to us about those matters *publicly* and *collectively*.

A more serious problem with Mysticism is that it offers no way, in principle, for us to judge between conflicting claims about what

## WORLDVIEWS

God expects of us or requires of us. If Jack says God told him one thing while Jill says God told her the very opposite, how can we determine which (if either) of them is right? Surely we need some *public* and *objective* way of confirming what God has actually communicated to us.

Suppose, for example, I claim that God spoke to me directly and told me that I should take your new sports car for a spin and then sacrifice your pet hamster as a burnt offering. How can you prove otherwise? It won't do to complain that God didn't tell *you* those things! If God only speaks to people privately and individually, you have no basis for contesting what I claim about God's will. It will always be my word against yours.

Here's the upshot. If God's most important communications with humans aren't a matter of public record—if God hasn't spoken in a way that, in principle, anyone can access, understand, and confirm—then there's really no way for anyone to verify or judge between conflicting claims about what God has actually said.

Imagine what it would be like to live in a country where the founding constitution and laws of the nation have never been publicly communicated and recorded. How well would *that* work? Practical anarchy would be the result.

In the same way, Mysticism seems to lead inevitably to *religious* anarchy—and perhaps *moral* anarchy, as well. Is that the sort of situation that God wants us to be in?

You've reached the end of the trail. However:

**To reconsider the Openness Question, go to page 35.**
**To reconsider the Communication Question, go to page 34.**

# Worldview: Nihilism

Nihilism (from the Latin word *nihil*, meaning "nothing") is the view that there are no objective values: nothing is really good or bad in any objective sense. In particular, there are no objective *moral* values. According to Nihilism, nothing is ultimately right or wrong, good or bad, justified or unjustified. What's more, there is no objective purpose or meaning in human life or the universe at large. There's simply no right or wrong way to live your life. Whatever you choose to do is just as valuable—or, rather, just as *valueless*—as anything else you might choose to do.

For the bona fide Nihilist, if you were to put down this book and throw yourself off the nearest tall building, that decision would be no better or worse, in any objective sense, than continuing to read this book. Ultimately, it really doesn't matter one way or the other. You may *prefer* to do one rather than the other (I hope it's the second option!), but for the Nihilist, no human preference is more or less valuable than any other human preference.

According to Nihilism, then, everything just is what it is: end of story. There's no right or wrong about it. Beyond our arbitrary personal preferences, there's nothing good to pursue and nothing bad to avoid. Our moral questions literally have no real answers. As the Cole Porter song famously put it, "Anything goes!"

Nihilism clearly isn't a very attractive or appealing viewpoint, but that doesn't mean that it isn't true. Indeed, often the truth turns out to be quite different than we want it to be! Nevertheless, Nihilism faces two formidable objections that make it very hard to accept on a rational basis.

The first objection is that Nihilism conflicts with our strongest moral intuitions. Most people recognize that some things are just plain wrong, no matter what. For example, torturing and murdering children for sadistic pleasure is *objectively* wrong. Even if everyone in the world enjoyed it and wanted to do it, it would still be wrong. Some moral values really are independent of human preferences.

Of course, the Nihilist might insist that our moral intuitions are completely unreliable and should be disregarded. But we would need to have *very* good reasons to dismiss such strong and widely held intuitions. Are there reasons to embrace Nihilism that are more obvious to us than our moral intuitions? And if our *moral* intuitions are so thoroughly misleading, why should we trust any of our *other* intuitions? Why should we trust our *rational* intuitions? Nihilism threatens to undermine our rationality just as much as it undermines our morality.

This leads to a second and even more devastating objection to Nihilism: it's self-defeating. Presumably the Nihilist thinks that it's *rational* to accept Nihilism. (Why would you believe something if you thought it wasn't rational to believe it?) But when we say that a belief is "rational," we're making a value judgment about it, at least implicitly. When we distinguish between rational beliefs and irrational beliefs, we're essentially distinguishing between good beliefs and bad beliefs. But if Nihilism is true, there's nothing objectively good or bad about any beliefs! Whatever you happen to believe is just as valuable or, rather, just as valueless as anything else you might believe.

Therefore, a truly consistent Nihilist should say that there's no objective distinction between rational beliefs and irrational beliefs. When it comes to beliefs, as with morality, "Anything goes!"

So if you're a consistent Nihilist, why do you believe Nihilism? Whatever explanation you give, it can't have anything to do with trying to be rational in your beliefs.

You've reached the end of the trail. However:

**To reconsider the Goodness Question, go to page 23.**

# Worldview: Non-Mainstream Monotheism

It isn't the catchiest of labels, but "Non-Mainstream Monotheism" is one way to describe the worldview that fits your answers to the questions. According to this worldview, there is a personal and perfect God who created and sustains the universe, and who has communicated with human beings in an open and public way, but not in the way claimed by any of the three main Monotheist religions: Christianity, Islam, and Judaism. People who hold this worldview might *describe* themselves as Christians, Muslims, or Jews, but they reject one or more of the central claims of those religions. They also deny that any of the holy books of those religions—the Bible, the Qur'an, or the Tanach—should be accepted as divine revelation.

One major challenge faced by Non-Mainstream Monotheism is that it represents a peculiar "minority report." Your answers to the questions indicate that you believe that God is a personal and perfect Supreme Being who has communicated with us openly and publicly. But if that communication isn't the Bible, the Qur'an, or the Tanach, what is it? If it really is a public divine revelation, why have so few people in history recognized it? To adapt a line from the movie *Cool Hand Luke*, what we've got here is a divine failure to communicate.

Non-Mainstream Monotheists might not want to *completely* reject those holy books. They might say that God has spoken through *parts* of those books, but the other parts should be rejected as merely human opinions. Yet that raises a tricky question: How do you reliably separate the wheat from the chaff? Unless you have some kind of direct insight into the mind of God, how could you be in any position to determine which parts of those books are *really* from him? This leads to another question: Why would an all-good, all-wise, all-powerful God use such a confusing and unreliable method of communication in the first place? To use a radio analogy: Why would God allow his signal to get so swamped by noise?

Non-Mainstream Monotheism may be a minority position among Theist worldviews, but that alone doesn't imply that it's mistaken. Sometimes the minority view turns out to be correct. At one time, for example, only a minority of people believed that the Earth orbits the sun rather than the reverse. But when you consider all the implications of a Theist worldview, including what it implies about a public divine revelation, Non-Mainstream Monotheism seems difficult to defend.

It's also important to recognize that this worldview doesn't represent a single unified alternative to Christianity, Islam, and Judaism. On the contrary, there's considerable disagreement among Non-Mainstream Monotheists as to exactly how and where God has communicated! So this "minority report" actually turns out to be a *plurality* of "minority reports," each one competing against the others. How do we discriminate between all these different viewpoints within Non-Mainstream Monotheism?

The challenge faced by each one of these viewpoints shouldn't be underestimated. When it comes to competing claims about a public divine revelation, this principle seems to apply: the less common the viewpoint, the greater the burden of proof it bears.

In the end, Non-Mainstream Monotheism raises more questions than it answers.

You've reached the end of the trail. However:

**To reconsider the Moses Question, go to page 38.**
**To reconsider the Muhammad Question, go to page 37.**
**To reconsider the Resurrection Question, go to page 36.**

# Worldview: Panentheism

Panentheism (from the Greek words *pan*, *en*, and *theos*, literally "all-in-God") is the view that God encompasses everything that exists, including the universe we inhabit, but there is more to God than just the universe. Panentheism shouldn't be confused with Pantheism, which says that God and the universe are one and the same: the universe *is* God. In contrast, Panentheism maintains that the universe is a *part* of God, not the whole.

Panentheists often suggest that the relationship between God and the universe is similar to the relationship between you and your body. Your body is only part of you; there's more to you than your body. You have a physical aspect (the body) and a mental or spiritual aspect (the mind or soul). Similarly, God has a physical aspect (the natural universe) and a mental or spiritual aspect (God's mind or soul, which animates and directs the universe).

Another idea commonly associated with Panentheism is that God is *dependent* on the universe. As one influential Panentheist put it, "Without the world, God is not God."[39] Just as humans need a physical body in order to be complete, God needs the natural universe in order to be complete.

Panentheism is most commonly found among Eastern religions, particularly Hinduism. (Strictly speaking, Hinduism is more of a *family* of religions rather than one religion; some forms of Hinduism are Panentheist, while others are not.) The Hare Krishna movement, which has its roots in Hinduism, is often thought to favor a Panentheist worldview.

Panentheism has some attractive features, particularly for those who can't stomach the nihilistic consequences of Atheist worldviews (see page 43). It also avoids some of the problems associated with Pantheism (see page 81). Even so, Pantheism and Panentheism face one serious problem together: the reality of evil in the universe.

If there is real evil within the universe—hatred, slavery, genocide, famine, and so on—then there must be real evil *within God*, for according to Panentheism, the entire universe is within God. As I noted earlier, Panentheists have suggested that the universe is something like a part of God. But then it seems to follow that God must be *partly evil*: there is some part of God's being that is evil, precisely because there is some part of the universe that is evil. If the universe isn't purely good, neither can God be purely good. But can a God that is less than purely good be worthy of the title "God"?

This leads directly to another problem. If God is the ultimate standard of goodness (as you'd expect God to be), it seems a Panentheist has to say that the ultimate standard of goodness isn't *purely* good. But that doesn't make a lot of sense. By what standard could the ultimate standard of goodness be judged less than purely good? There can't be a *higher* standard of goodness than the *ultimate* standard!

The Panentheist might reply that God isn't the ultimate standard of goodness after all. There's some higher standard of goodness by which the universe, and therefore God, can be judged less than purely good. But if that's the case, wouldn't that higher standard of goodness be more worthy of the title "God"?

In sum, Panentheism struggles to reconcile the absolute goodness of God with its claim that the entire universe is within God. It seems that the only way to preserve the absolute goodness of God is to maintain that God is *distinct* from the universe.

You've reached the end of the trail. However:

**To reconsider the All-In-God Question, go to page 31.**
**To reconsider the All-Is-God Question, go to page 30.**
**To reconsider the Personality Question, go to page 29.**

# Worldview: Pantheism

Pantheism (from the Greek words *pan* and *theos*, literally "all-God") is the view that there is a God, and God is *everything*. For the Pantheist, God isn't beyond the universe or greater than the universe. Rather, God *is* the universe. In other words, the universe is literally divine. One attractive implication of this worldview is that you and I are God—or at least part of God! (You can imagine what a boost in self-esteem this can provide.)

Pantheism is far more common in Eastern cultures than in Western cultures. For example, certain forms of Hinduism, Buddhism, and Taoism are explicitly Pantheist. However, Pantheism has made significant inroads to the West in recent years through the New Age movement and the modern revival of paganism.

Despite its prominence in some cultures, Pantheism faces serious problems as a worldview, at least for those who believe in the reality of good and evil. (Recall that you answered yes to the Goodness Question.) I noted earlier that one of the advantages of Theist worldviews is that they can account for a real objective distinction between good and evil. God is the source and standard of all goodness. Goodness is ultimately *godliness*.

But this raises quite a problem for a Pantheist. If everything is *God*, then it seems to follow that everything is *good*. If God is pure goodness—as surely God ought to be—then every part of God must be good. I'm good; you're good; we're all good. Adolf Hitler was good. The Holocaust was good. Child abuse is good. Cancer is good. It's all good, because it's all *God*.

Pantheism is often associated with Monism (see page 71). Monism is the view that everything is ultimately one; all distinctions are ultimately illusory. For those who think that God must be a pure unity, Pantheism leads directly to Monism: if all is God and God is one, then all is one. While many Pantheists are happy to take this step, Monism makes it even harder to accept the reality of evil, because a consistent Monist has to reject as illusory any ultimate distinction between good and evil.

## WORLDVIEWS

But even for Pantheists who don't accept Monism, there seems to be no logical place for genuine evil in their worldview. Pantheism may seem attractive on the surface—who wouldn't want to be part of God?—but on reflection it has very implausible and unpalatable implications. For the Pantheist, the problem of evil becomes the problem of the *denial* of evil.

If you hold to a Pantheist worldview, are you willing to say that ultimately everything is good and nothing is evil? Perhaps you are. But can you walk the talk as well? Can you live consistently with that consequence of your worldview?

You've reached the end of the trail. However:

**To reconsider the All-Is-God Question, go to page 30.**
**To reconsider the Personality Question, go to page 29.**
**To reconsider the God Question, go to page 25.**

# Worldview: Pelagianism

You might think that any Theist who believes that God has spoken through the Bible and that Jesus is the divine Son of God who rose from the dead must be a Christian. Strictly speaking, however, that isn't the case, because there's at least one more idea that is central to Christianity and distinguishes it from other religious worldviews—including the one we've ended up with here: Pelagianism.

Pelagianism gets its name from Pelagius, a monk who lived in Rome in the fifth century. Pelagius taught that humans enter this world completely untainted by sin and with perfect freedom to choose between good and evil. We aren't *born* sinful, but we can *become* sinful by failing to follow God's moral laws and Christ's moral example. Pelagius held that heaven is basically the reward for a good life. If you follow the example of Jesus and live a good moral life, you'll receive eternal life. God's help ("divine grace") is available for those who need it, but the basic principle is that the way to get to heaven is by doing your level best to love God and love others. In other words, divine grace isn't strictly needed to get to heaven—and the less you fall back on it the better!

Pelagius claimed to be following the teachings of Jesus, but his views caused an uproar in the early Christian church because, in effect, he was denying the clear teaching of the New Testament that salvation is entirely a free gift of God. According to the Bible, we're saved "by grace alone" and not because we live good lives.[40] As the apostle Paul put it, sin earns us death, but eternal life is the gift of God in Jesus Christ.[41]

Unpopular though the idea may be today, the Bible teaches the polar opposite of Pelagianism: we are born in a sinful and spiritually dead state, unable to live good moral lives apart from divine grace.[42] Indeed, Jesus himself preached the shocking idea that heaven is for immoral people who admit that they're bad and cry out for God's mercy and forgiveness rather than for moral people who think they're good enough to deserve it.[43]

## WORLDVIEWS

It's not so surprising, then, that Pelagianism was condemned as heresy by the entire Christian church at a council in AD 431. Remarkably, however, there are many people today who consider themselves Christians but are actually closer to Pelagius when it comes to their beliefs about who gets to heaven and on what basis. Pelagianism says that we're all born good, and if we stay good enough we'll receive eternal life as our reward. In stark contrast, Christianity says that we're all born bad, but bad people can still obtain eternal life—not because we deserve it in the least, but because out of his great love and mercy God offers it as a gift to those who put their trust in Jesus Christ.[44]

You've reached the end of the trail. However:

**To reconsider the Salvation Question, go to page 40.**
**To reconsider the Divinity Question, go to page 39.**
**To reconsider the Resurrection Question, go to page 36.**

# Worldview: Platonism

Platonism, as I'm using the term, is the view that there are two distinct and radically different realms of reality. The first (lower) realm is material, changeable, transient, and accessible via our senses; it is what we usually call the natural or physical universe. The second (higher) realm is immaterial, unchangeable, eternal, and not accessible via our senses. (Platonism is named after the ancient Greek philosopher Plato, who defended something like this two-level view of reality.)

According to Platonism, what we call "God" is essentially the highest principle of truth, goodness, and beauty in the transcendent realm, and things in the material realm are true, good, and beautiful to the extent they conform to God. For the Platonist, God is the highest of all things, perfect in every respect and utterly transcendent. God is quite distinct from the universe; the universe isn't *within* God. However, God isn't a *personal* being. God is more like an impersonal divine principle or abstract ideal.

Platonism holds a significant advantage over other worldviews (such as Atheism, Panentheism, and Pantheism) because it posits an absolute, objective standard of goodness that is distinct from the universe. The universe is a *mixture* of good and evil (as the newspapers confirm for us every day), but God is not. So on the face of it, Platonism gives a plausible explanation as to why there are real, objective distinctions between good and evil, truth and falsity, and so forth. There is an ultimate standard of truth, goodness, and beauty—namely, God—and things in our universe (including us) are good or bad to the extent that they conform to this standard.

However, Platonism faces a host of questions that turn out to be rather tough to answer. Why does the material universe exist in the first place? How are these two radically different realms connected? How can one influence the other?

According to most Theists, God is a personal being with intellect, intentions, free will, and causal powers. God has thoughts and plans, he makes free choices, and he has the power to influence other things—to create them, sustain them, change them, direct them, and so forth. The problem for Platonism is that an impersonal principle or abstract ideal doesn't have any of these capacities or powers. So the Platonist can't readily explain why an orderly material universe exists at all, why it bears the marks of intelligent design and contains personal beings like us, and why human life has meaning, purpose, and moral direction. These specific features of our universe are far less surprising if God is a powerful personal being.

On a more practical level, why should we believe for a moment that Platonism's God cares in the slightest about what happens in our universe and in our lives? (Can an impersonal, transcendent principle of goodness "care" about *anything*?) If we're irrelevant to God, why should God be relevant to us?

Platonism may have its virtues, but many people find it less philosophically and religiously satisfying than a Theist worldview in which God is understood to be a *personal* Supreme Being.

You've reached the end of the trail. However:

**To reconsider the All-In-God Question, go to page 31.**
**To reconsider the All-Is-God Question, go to page 30.**
**To reconsider the Personality Question, go to page 29.**

# Worldview: Pluralism

Pluralism is the view that there is more than one valid religion. There is an ultimate reality, but no single religion has a monopoly on the truth about that reality. Each religion represents a different but legitimate perspective on it. Each religion has a distinctive understanding of "God," "truth," "enlightenment," "salvation," and so on, and they are all valid. In the same way, Pluralism insists that no single religion holds a monopoly on how we are to be "saved." As an ancient saying puts it, "There are many paths up the mountain."

Pluralism is a relative newcomer in the history of worldviews, but it's becoming increasingly widespread, particularly as people grow tired of religious violence and intolerance. Pluralism advocates a "live and let live" attitude, promoting tolerance toward all religious traditions (or at least toward *most* of them).

Appealing as it may seem in our day, Pluralism faces some serious problems. First, there's the fact that the major religions make central claims that are logically incompatible. Christianity teaches that Jesus was the divine Son of God, but Islam explicitly and vehemently rejects that claim. Judaism holds that God is personal, but many forms of Hinduism teach that God is non-personal. Some forms of Buddhism affirm no God at all. Clearly these aren't minor disagreements that can be swept under the carpet! These distinctive teachings lie at the very heart of these religions.

Even so, Pluralists think they have an answer to this problem. They often suggest that such conflicts can be resolved by taking all these religious claims *figuratively* rather than *literally*. For example, when Christians say, "The Bible is the Word of God," we shouldn't interpret it as a claim that God literally speaks to people through the Bible. It's only a figurative way of saying that Christians happen to find reading the Bible spiritually edifying and enlightening—or something along those lines. Understood in that figurative sense, the sacred scriptures of the major religions could all be described as "the Word of God." No more conflicts!

The trouble with this line is that it doesn't accurately reflect what the adherents of those religions themselves mean by these claims. In effect, Pluralists are suggesting that Buddhists, Hindus, Jews, Muslims, Christians, and so on are actually quite mistaken about how to understand their own religions. Are we to believe that they have less understanding of the teachings of their own religions than modern Pluralists?

Think again about the analogy of the blind men and the elephant. (If you need a reminder, flip back to page 24.) Doesn't the analogy imply not only that traditional religious believers are actually quite mistaken about the overarching truth, but also that the Pluralist *alone* has the full and correct view of the ultimate reality in his role as the narrator of the story? It suggests that the Pluralist has a uniquely privileged insight that everyone else lacks.

On closer examination, Pluralism turns out to be just as "exclusive" and "intolerant" as many traditional religions, if not more so, simply because it cannot accommodate any religion that rejects its distinctive perspective on religion. If Pluralism is right, other religions must be quite wrong. So much for "live and let live"! By excluding non-Pluralist religions, Pluralism exposes itself as just one more religious viewpoint in competition with all the others.

In the end, it's hard to defend the view that there are *many* valid religions. The conflicting teachings of the major world religions can't be harmonized without distorting those religions beyond recognition. At least some of these religious teachings must be mistaken, which means that some religions have a better handle on the truth about the ultimate reality than others. In fact, it's reasonable to suppose that one particular religion has the *best* handle on the truth, all things considered.

So the question becomes: Which one?

You've reached the end of the trail. However:

**To reconsider the Religion Question, go to page 24.**

# Worldview: Polytheism

Polytheism (from the Greek words *polus* and *theos*, literally "many gods") is simply the view that there are multiple deities. Polytheism has to be classified as a Finite Theist worldview because if there are many gods, they have to be finite and limited in power. (Think it through: there can't be multiple all-powerful beings because each one would have the power to defeat every other one, in which case they wouldn't be all-powerful after all.)

Polytheists typically believe that the gods exist *within* the natural universe rather than transcending it. That helps to explain why the gods are limited: they're constrained by the natural laws of the universe.

The ancient Greeks and Romans held to this form of Polytheism, as did many other ancient cultures. It's less well known that Mormonism also represents a Polytheist worldview. According to the traditional teachings of the Church of Jesus Christ of Latter-day Saints, there are many gods, and those gods were once human beings. As one Mormon apostle, John A. Widtsoe, famously put it, "Man is a god in embryo."[45] So gods are nothing less than exalted human beings. But since humans are physical beings, so are the gods. They're limited by the basic physical laws of the universe, just as we are.

Polytheism has cropped up many times in the history of mankind, but it isn't a very philosophically satisfying worldview because it has no good answers to some very basic questions. Where did the gods come from? Where did the universe come from, and why does it have the laws it has if the gods didn't create it? (Remember that Polytheists typically believe that the gods are part of the universe—they exist *within* it—so they can't have created it.)

Another problem for Polytheism is connected to your answer to the Goodness Question. You said that some things are *objectively* good or bad, which implies that there is an ultimate standard of goodness. Where does it come from?

For the Monotheist, who believes in one absolute and infinite

## WORLDVIEWS

God, it's obvious that God must be the ultimate standard of goodness. One God, one ultimate standard. No problem!

But the Polytheist faces an awkward question at this point: *Which God?* If there are multiple gods, doesn't that mean there are multiple standards of goodness? If so, it looks as if the Polytheist must settle for relativism or arbitrariness when it comes to the ultimate standard. ("Pick a god, any god!") There's also the tricky question of which god to worship and obey.

Of course, the Polytheist may prefer to say that *no* god is the ultimate standard of goodness. Rather, the ultimate standard of goodness is distinct from all the gods and transcends them. But in that case, wouldn't that ultimate standard be the Supreme Being, since it transcends the gods and stands over them? It seems the Polytheist has to deny that there's any ultimate standard or he isn't really a Polytheist after all.

You've reached the end of the trail. However:

**To reconsider the Uniqueness Question, go to page 33.**
**To reconsider the Perfection Question, go to page 32.**
**To reconsider the Personality Question, go to page 29.**

# Worldview: Relativism

Relativism is the view that there is no *objective* truth. According to Relativism, there are no beliefs or claims that are simply true period, regardless of what anyone happens to think, hope, or feel about them.

Relativists insist that what we call "truth" is always *relative* to something else. There are basically two kinds of Relativist. The first kind—the Subjectivist—claims that truth is always relative to the individual person. So the Subjectivist talks about what's "true for me" and what's "true for you"—and these two "truths" needn't be the same. For example, while it may be true for me that the universe has meaning and purpose, it might not be true for you.

The second kind of Relativist—the Cultural Relativist—doesn't claim that truth is relative to the individual person, but he does claim that it is relative to that person's culture or society. So the Cultural Relativist might talk about what was "true for the ancient Greeks" as opposed to what is "true for modern Americans"—and those two "truths" needn't be the same. Or he might talk about what is true for people in different religious communities. For example, while it may be "true for Christians" that Jesus is God, it isn't "true for Buddhists."

It's important to understand that Relativism (of both kinds) isn't saying only that people have different beliefs or ideas. It isn't claiming merely that what one person or culture thinks is true may not be the same as what some other person or culture thinks is true. No one would deny that! Relativists are making a far more radical and controversial claim, namely, that *truth itself* varies from person to person or from culture to culture. In other words, a genuine Relativist denies even that there are objective facts about reality that must be the same for everyone, everywhere. For the full-fledged Relativist, "facts" are just as relative as "truths."

Relativism is surprisingly widespread in our day, but in all its forms it faces two crippling problems. The first is that it flies in the face of our basic intuitions about truth. How credible is it to think, for example, that the statement "Dynamite is explosive" could be true for some people but not for others? (Would you be willing to put that theory to the test?) Could a statement such as "The planet Earth has one moon" really be true for people in one culture but not for people in another culture?

Surely the same principle applies to religious claims such as "The universe was created by a personal God" and "God has spoken through human prophets." Either they're true or they're not true. Whether those claims are true or not depends on objective facts about reality, not on personal opinions or cultural conventions.

The second and even more serious problem is that Relativism is self-defeating. There's no way to be a *consistent* Relativist. Just consider the basic claim of Relativism: "There is no objective truth." Is that claim *itself* supposed to be objectively true? If so, it obviously contradicts itself! But if the basic claim of Relativism *isn't* objectively true, Relativism seems to forfeit any right to be universally accepted or meaningfully debated. It makes no sense for Relativists to say, "We're right about truth and everyone else is wrong," because that statement implies there's an objectively true answer to the question "Who's right about truth?"

In other words, Relativism ultimately trivializes disagreements, including the disagreement between Relativists and non-Relativists. If truth is always relative, then it's not possible for there to be real disagreements between individuals (for the Subjectivist) or between cultures (for the Cultural Relativist). For the Relativist, *everyone* can be right—relatively! But that means non-Relativists can be just as right as Relativists—which doesn't seem right to anyone.

In the end, it's hard to deny that there really is objective truth.

You've reached the end of the trail. However:

**To reconsider the Truth Question, go to page 21.**

# Worldview: Skepticism

Skepticism is the view that even if there is objective truth, none of us can *know* what that truth is. Skeptics think that our minds simply aren't equipped to determine the truth with any degree of confidence. If anyone claims to know the truth, he's kidding himself. Skeptics are thus the champions of doubt; if nothing can be known to be true, then everything is subject to doubt.

Skepticism is perhaps more widespread in our day than ever before, but the view has been around for thousands of years. The ancient Greek philosopher Pyrrho, who was born in the fourth century BC, is often credited with being the first Skeptic. He thought that our senses shouldn't be trusted and therefore we can never know that things in the world really are what they appear to be. In other words, none of us can know the objective truth about the world. And since we can't know the truth, Pyrrho argued, we should try to suspend judgment about everything. If someone makes a truth claim, we should neither believe it nor disbelieve it. We shouldn't consider one person's opinion to be any closer to the truth than any other person's.

At first, Skepticism appears to be a thoroughly humble viewpoint. What could be more humble than saying you don't know anything? What could be more modest than considering your opinion no better than anyone else's? In reality, however, Skepticism is remarkably bold—even arrogant—because it makes sweeping claims about the capacity of the human mind that it can't consistently support.

In effect, Skeptics want us to believe that they alone have discerned some universal truth about human knowledge, namely, that there isn't any human knowledge. But do they claim to *know* that? If they do, they're not being consistently skeptical; specifically, they're not being skeptical about their own claim to know a universal truth. On the other hand, if they say they *don't* know that Skepticism is correct, why should we take their position seriously? By their own profession, their opinions about human knowledge are no better than anyone else's!

We can identify two basic problems with Skepticism that make it hard to take seriously. In the first place, the general claim that we can't know *any* truth flies in the face of common sense and cannot be consistently maintained in practice. We all take for granted—indeed, we *have* to take for granted—that we know many important truths, including all of the following: (1) There is a real, objective world behind our sense experiences, a world that all of us inhabit. (2) This world has existed for more than ten minutes and will probably exist for at least another ten minutes. (3) This world operates in an orderly and predictable fashion, according to laws of nature. (4) Other people have conscious minds like our own, even though we can see only their bodies. (5) Our bodies can be directed by our minds. (6) There are moral principles that apply to us and to others. If we didn't know all these things, our everyday decisions and actions would be pointless and worthless.

The second problem is that Skepticism is self-defeating. If its central claim is true, then no one can *know* it's true! So why should anyone believe it? (If we follow Pyrrho's advice, we should neither believe it nor disbelieve it.) Ironically, if you think that Skepticism is more reasonable than non-Skepticism, then you ought to reject Skepticism precisely because it denies that any one viewpoint is more reasonable than another! If you want to be a consistent Skeptic, you should be as doubtful about Skepticism as you are about everything else.

Skepticism doesn't just make a strong claim about knowledge. It makes *too* strong a claim. We certainly don't know *everything*, but it makes little sense to say that we don't know *anything*. Skepticism is hard to defend and even harder to live out consistently in practice.

You've reached the end of the trail. However:

**To reconsider the Knowledge Question, go to page 22.**

# Worldview: Unitarianism

Unitarianism is the view that there is only one God—the Supreme Being whom Jesus referred to as "Father"—and that Jesus himself was *not* divine, at least not in any literal sense. Jews and Muslims believe that there is only one God and that Jesus was a mere human being like the rest of us, but unlike Unitarians, they don't claim to be followers of Jesus. Unitarians may also believe that Jesus was raised from the dead, which would further distinguish them from Jews and Muslims.

Unitarians may accept the New Testament as divinely revealed scripture, but they reject the doctrine of the Trinity, the teaching that God exists in three distinct persons: the Father, the Son (Jesus), and the Holy Spirit. They also reject the doctrine of the incarnation, according to which Jesus is a divine person who has existed eternally but became a human being in order to save his people from their sins.[46]

Unitarians typically argue that the doctrines of the Trinity and the incarnation don't make logical sense and therefore shouldn't be accepted. But Unitarianism faces two sticky problems: the New Testament and early Christianity.

The first problem for Unitarianism is that the writers of the New Testament, some of whom were among Jesus's first disciples, undoubtedly believed that there is only one God, yet they also referred to Jesus as God.[47] What's more, they said things about Jesus that could be true only if he is divine; for example, that he existed before the creation of the universe and was instrumental in its creation.[48] Most significant of all, Jesus *himself* said things that implied he was equal with God, with the result that he was charged with blasphemy by his fellow Jews, who were all strict Monotheists.[49] On one occasion, they tried to stone him to death for that very reason.

The second problem for Unitarianism is that the history of early Christianity reinforces this view of Jesus. To give just one example: Ignatius of Antioch, a Christian bishop at the beginning of the second century, wrote a number of letters to Christians in other cities, and in these letters he explicitly affirmed the divinity of Jesus. For example, several times Ignatius referred to Jesus as "our God," and he clearly assumed that those to whom he was writing shared his view of Jesus.

In addition to all this, we know for a fact that the early Christians *worshiped* Jesus.[50] Yet they also accepted the Old Testament, which clearly teaches that only the one true God should be worshiped![51] They understood very well that it would be sheer blasphemous idolatry to worship a mere human being—to worship a creature rather than the Creator.[52] Incredibly, however, that didn't stop them worshiping Jesus. This historical fact makes sense only if these early Christians believed that Jesus was nothing less than divine. It's quite telling that some of the early Christians were so convinced of the divinity of Jesus that they weren't sure whether he was really *human*!

So Unitarians who claim to accept the Bible and to represent genuine Christianity have to deal with the awkward fact that the New Testament and early Christianity point in a very different direction. Unitarians may have their reasons for rejecting the doctrines of the Trinity and the incarnation, but if they want to be consistent, it seems they ought to reject the Jesus of the New Testament as well.

You've reached the end of the trail. However:

**To reconsider the Divinity Question, go to page 39.**
**To reconsider the Resurrection Question, go to page 36.**

# Appendix

QUESTIONS AND ANSWERS

**1. Okay, I've figured out what worldview I have. What now?**
There are several things you can do to deepen your understanding of your worldview.

First, you can spend some time reflecting on the objections and challenges faced by your worldview, starting with the ones I've highlighted in this book. How serious are those objections and challenges? Are they fair criticisms? How would you respond to them? Does your worldview face any other criticisms or difficulties that you need to think about more deeply? How do the most thoughtful and sophisticated advocates of your worldview deal with the major objections and challenges?

Second, you could consider whether you actually live in a way that's consistent with your worldview. Given your worldview, does it make sense to live the way you do? How *should* people with your worldview live in order to be consistent with that worldview? What should be their goals and priorities? How should they relate to other people?

If it turns out that you *don't* live in a way consistent with your worldview, ask yourself: Why not? Is it because *no one* could possibly live in a way consistent with that worldview? (If so, that may be a black mark against your worldview!) Or is it because you don't take your worldview as seriously as you should?

Many people today suffer from a disconnect between what they say they believe (or think they believe) and what their lifestyle suggests about their real convictions—or lack of them! So it's worth pondering this question: Does your day-to-day life reflect a different worldview than the one you think you have?

Third, I encourage you to explore the many other paths in this book to see where you would have ended up had you answered the questions differently. What other worldviews are out there? At what points do they significantly differ from your worldview? Do they compare favorably or unfavorably with your worldview? How reasonable and coherent are they, all things considered? Do they face more or fewer problems than your worldview? Do they make better sense of everything we take for granted in our experience of the world? Do they make better sense of the course of human history? Do they offer good answers to the "big questions" of human existence?

The best way to assess the strengths and weaknesses of your worldview is to compare it to the alternatives, being as objective and critical as you can. I hope you'll find this book a useful tool in that regard.

## 2. Isn't all this rather superficial and simplistic?

The content of this book is *simplified*, certainly, but I don't believe it's *simplistic*. It has to be simplified because it isn't possible to discuss every aspect of every worldview while still keeping the book short and engaging. But it isn't simplistic, because the book asks the most important questions that need to be asked, it covers the most prominent and influential worldviews in Western culture today (plus a few more), and it highlights some of the most serious challenges faced by those worldviews. The book doesn't drill down all the way, but it certainly digs below the surface of our everyday thoughts and activities to explore what lies beneath.

I want to emphasize that this book isn't meant to be the last word on worldviews—not by a long shot! Rather, it's meant to be the first word in a fruitful conversation about matters of ultimate importance. My goal in this book isn't to persuade readers to agree with my views. (If it does persuade you, well, that's a bonus!) But if the book provokes you to think more self-consciously and critically about your worldview and the worldviews of others, it has done exactly what it was designed to accomplish.

Appendix

### 3. Aren't there other worldviews one could have?

Yes and no! Let me explain.

Just as there's more than one way to slice a cake, the field of worldviews can be divided up in many ways, and this book reflects only one way of doing so. For example, some of the worldviews identified in the book, such as Panentheism, could be *further* divided: I could have discussed several *types* of Panentheist worldviews.

However, the book is designed for a particular readership in a particular culture. It aims to cover all of the prominent and influential worldviews in Western culture today. The selection of questions asked (and the order in which they're asked) aims to distinguish between these worldviews in the most economical way.

In addition, it's important to see that the particular worldviews mentioned in this book, when taken together, ought to cover the field of worldviews completely. That's because all the questions asked in the book are *closed binary* questions, which simply means that they have only two possible correct answers: yes and no. Take the God Question for example. Either there is a God (as defined on the question page) or there isn't. There's no other possible *correct* answer to the question. The same goes for all the other questions. This means that as you follow the trail through the book, every fork in the path presents only two possible routes forward, and the worldview at the end of each trail is precisely the worldview that best fits the answers to all the questions that led to it.

Whatever worldview you have, then, should be represented somewhere in this book, even if the label I've used isn't exactly the label you would use. Your worldview may be included under some more general worldview (such as Materialism or Pantheism), but I'm confident that it is represented somewhere. In that respect, there are no other worldviews *besides* those identified in the book.

### 4. Aren't there problems you haven't mentioned?

Yes, of course. Each of the worldviews I discuss in the book faces more challenges and objections than I've mentioned. It would be impossible to touch on all of them in a book of this length. But I've tried to focus on some of the most serious challenges and objections to each worldview. If you think I've missed the mark in that regard, I'm glad to hear it, because it shows that you're thinking critically about worldviews—and that's exactly what the book is meant to encourage!

## 5. What's the difference between a worldview and a religion?

As I defined it in the introduction, a worldview is simply a person's overall philosophical view of the world. It's an all-encompassing perspective on everything that exists and matters to us. Your worldview shapes what you believe and what you're willing to believe, how you interpret your experiences, how you behave in response to those experiences, and how you relate to others.

A religion, on the other hand, is a set of fundamental beliefs and practices concerned with ultimate issues, such as the nature of the divine, the origins of the universe, the meaning of human existence, how we should live our lives and relate to one another, whether there is life after death, what it means to be "saved," and how we can obtain "salvation." Religions take many forms, but they typically involve teachings about how God relates to the universe and to us, adherence to certain sacred writings, observance of traditional rites and practices, symbols, moral codes, recognized leaders, and a strong sense of community. The major world religions today include Christianity, Islam, Hinduism, Buddhism, Confucianism, Sikhism, Judaism, Jainism, and the Baha'i Faith.

Everyone has a worldview, but not everyone has a religion. Atheists, for example, have worldviews but don't follow any religion. (Some have argued that even Atheists are religious, but while it's true that Atheists have beliefs about religion and about many of the "ultimate issues" mentioned above, they aren't religious in the conventional sense of the term.)

Also, while not every worldview represents a religion, every major world religion reflects *some* worldview or other, because each one has something to say about how we should view ourselves, others, the universe, and the divine. In other words, every major world religion offers answers—whether explicit or implicit—to the sort of fundamental questions posed throughout this book.

## 6. Why don't you mention such-and-such a religion?

This book is primarily about worldviews (hence the title!) rather than religions. So the book doesn't directly discuss every religion or even every *major* religion. (For an explanation of the difference between a worldview and a religion, see the answer to question 5 above.)

If a religion isn't mentioned explicitly in this book, that's probably for one of two reasons: either that religion doesn't hold a very prominent place in Western culture today (so not many readers of this book follow that religion) or that religion shares a major worldview with several other religions (so it makes more sense to cover those religions indirectly under that major worldview).

That said, every major religion should be *represented* somewhere in this book, either directly or indirectly, because each one reflects *some* worldview, and the book is designed to cover all the major worldviews in Western culture (see the answer to question 3 above). For example, many Eastern religions are represented by Panentheism and Pantheism, as are most forms of Neo-Paganism and New Age spirituality. The Church of Jesus Christ of Latter-day Saints (Mormonism) reflects the worldview of Polytheism, while the Watchtower Society (Jehovah's Witnesses) is represented by Unitarianism. Jainism is commonly understood to be Polytheist, whereas Sikhism clearly affirms a Monotheist worldview.

The upshot is this: no matter which religion you follow—or don't follow—you still have a worldview that should be represented somewhere in this book.

## 7. Isn't this all rigged to favor one particular worldview?

As I admitted in the introduction, I have my own worldview and therefore my own bias, just as you have yours. I believe that my worldview is correct, just as you believe that yours is correct (or at least more likely to be correct than the alternatives). I have my reasons for holding the worldview that I do, just as you have yours. The difference between us, however, is that I wrote this book and you didn't, which means that the book inevitably reflects my bias rather than yours—unless we both have the same worldview!

Since I believe that the worldview I hold makes better sense of the world than any of the alternatives, and that those other worldviews face more serious challenges and objections, it shouldn't be surprising to find that belief reflected in my comments on each worldview. Nevertheless, I haven't "rigged" the book in the sense that I have deliberately overstated the problems of some worldviews and understated or ignored the problems of others. (As I said in answer to questions 2 and 4 above, I recognize that there are many issues that I couldn't discuss without making the book much longer and less readable.) No worldview in this book gets a free pass! I'm well aware of the challenges faced by my own worldview and I've made a point of mentioning some of them along the way.

## 8. Does it really matter what worldview you have?

Yes, it really does. Your worldview is concerned with what you believe, and what you believe influences how you behave—and no one would say it doesn't matter how you behave. If it matters what you believe, then surely it matters what worldview you have, precisely because your worldview reflects your most significant and influential beliefs, and those beliefs have implications for almost everything else you believe. Your worldview concerns what you think about matters of ultimate importance, matters that affect your entire outlook on life. Your basic view of the world shapes how you *feel* about the world and how you *engage* with the world.

Dr. Martin Luther King Jr., the American civil rights leader, and Mao Tse-tung, the Chinese communist revolutionary leader, had very different worldviews, and their beliefs and actions were undoubtedly influenced in large measure by their worldviews. So does it really matter what worldview you have? Just ask those whose lives were changed for the better by the teachings of Dr. King or for the worse by the teachings of Chairman Mao.

It also matters what worldview you have because worldviews involve claims that can be true or false. Some worldviews have more truth in them than others. So if you care about truth, you ought to care about what worldview you have. You ought to seek out the worldview that is closest to the truth; the worldview that accurately reflects the way things really are; the worldview that allows us to see the world rightly. Having the wrong worldview is like wearing the wrong pair of spectacles: you won't see the world the way you *ought* to see it. None of us should want that!

## 9. Where can I learn more about these worldviews?

To learn more about the worldviews mentioned in this book, you can find further resources online at this address:

www.crossway.org/worldviewresources

# Notes

1. See the four Gospel accounts: Matthew 28, Mark 16, Luke 24, and John 20–21. Note especially the details given in Luke 24:36–43 and John 20:24–29.
2. Pliny the Younger, in a letter to the Emperor Trajan, dated around AD 112.
3. See John 1:1–14; John 3:13; John 8:58; John 17:5; Philippians 2:5–11; Colossians 1:15–17; Hebrews 1:1–12.
4. See Genesis 1:26–27; Matthew 22:37–40; James 3:9.
5. See Romans 1:1–4; 1 Corinthians 15:12–19.
6. See Mark 8:31; Mark 9:31; Mark 10:32–34, 45; John 5:18.
7. See Matthew 28:18; Mark 2:1–12; John 3:12–13; John 5:18; John 10:30.
8. See especially Luke 1:1–4 and John 21:24–25.
9. See Luke 24; John 20–21; Acts 1.
10. See Acts 2:14–36; Acts 8:26–35; Acts 13:26–41; Acts 17:1–4; Acts 18:24–28; Acts 26:22–23.
11. George Berkeley, *A Treatise Concerning the Principles of Human Knowledge* (Dublin: Aaron Rhames for Jeremy Pepyat, 1710), 3.
12. See John 1:29, 34; John 4:42; John 20:31.
13. See Genesis 1:1; Hebrews 11:3; Revelation 4:11.
14. See Genesis 1:26–27; James 3:9.
15. See Exodus 20:3–17 ("the Ten Commandments") and Matthew 22:37–40 ("the Two Great Commandments").
16. See Genesis 3:1–24; Romans 1:18–32.
17. See John 3:16–18; Romans 3:9–26; Romans 4:24–25; 1 Corinthians 15:1–8; Ephesians 2:1–10.
18. See Ephesians 2:20; Hebrews 1:1–2; 2 Peter 1:19–21.
19. See Matthew 11:29–30; Matthew 14:33; Matthew 28:9, 17; Mark 10:45; John 5:18; John 9:38; John 10:30.
20. See Matthew 5:48; Matthew 16:24; Matthew 19:21, 28–29; John 14:14; John 15:7.
21. See Matthew 5:20; Matthew 19:24–25; Matthew 21:28–32; Mark 2:17; Luke 18:9–14; Luke 23:39–42; John 3:3–5.

## Notes

22. See Matthew 8:20; Matthew 11:27; Matthew 28:18; John 6:15; John 18:36.
23. See Mark 4:35–41; Luke 7:11–17; Luke 8:40–56; John 11:17–44; John 18–19.
24. See Matthew 25:31–46; John 5:21–29; John 12:47.
25. The books of Moses, David, and Jesus are affirmed in the Qur'an: see Qur'an 3:3, 48; Qur'an 4:163; Qur'an 5:46, 66, 68, 110; Qur'an 9:111; Qur'an 17:55; Qur'an 21:105.
26. See Qur'an 2:81–82, 200–202; Qur'an 7:8–9, 40–42; Qur'an 9:20–22, 68; Qur'an 16:97; Qur'an 21:47; Qur'an 23:99–104; Qur'an 29:58; Qur'an 42:16–18; Qur'an 99:6–8; Qur'an 101:1–11.
27. See Qur'an 4:157–158, 171; Qur'an 19:35.
28. See Qur'an 6:34, 114–115; Qur'an 10:64; Qur'an 15:9; Qur'an 18:27.
29. See Qur'an 5:41–48, 65–68; Qur'an 7:157; Qur'an 10:94; Qur'an 16:43–44; Qur'an 21:7.
30. Codex Sinaiticus, which has survived with a large portion of the Old Testament and the entire New Testament, was written in the fourth century AD. Codex Alexandrinus, which has survived with most of the Old Testament and all of the books of the New Testament, has been dated to the fifth century AD. Both of these manuscripts are on display at the British Library in London. There are also ancient manuscripts containing significant portions of the Hebrew Bible that date to before the birth of Jesus.
31. See Matthew 16:13–20; Matthew 26:63–65; Luke 4:16–21. "Christ" is the Greek equivalent of "Messiah."
32. See Acts 2.
33. See Luke 4:16–21; Luke 24:13–27; Acts 2:14–36; Acts 3:17–26; Acts 7:1–53; Acts 8:26–35; Acts 13:16–41.
34. Some of the most significant messianic prophecies can be found in these Old Testament passages: Genesis 3:15; Psalm 2; Psalm 16; Psalm 22; Psalm 110; Isaiah 7:14; Isaiah 9:2–7; Isaiah 11:1–10; Isaiah 42:1–9; Isaiah 53; Jeremiah 23:5–6; Daniel 7:13–14; Micah 5:2; Zechariah 9:9; Zechariah 12:10.
35. The requirement to keep the laws and commandments of God is repeated over and over in Deuteronomy, the last of the five books of the Torah. For some examples, see the following verses: Deuteronomy 4:2, 40; Deuteronomy 6:17; Deuteronomy 8:6; Deuteronomy 11:1; Deuteronomy 30:8–10.
36. See Deuteronomy 27:26. The curses that would fall on the Israelites if they failed to obey all God's commandments are detailed in Deuteronomy 28:15–68.
37. See Galatians 3:10–14.

Notes

38. According to modern physics, matter is convertible into energy and vice versa. So modern Materialism allows for both.
39. G. W. F. Hegel, *Lectures on the Philosophy of Religion*, ed. and trans. Ebenezer Brown Speirs and J. Burdon Sanderson, 3 vols. (London: K. Paul, Trench, Trübner and Co., 1895), I:200.
40. See Romans 4:1–8; Romans 11:6; Ephesians 2:8–9.
41. See Romans 6:23.
42. See Romans 3:9–20; Romans 6:15–23; Ephesians 2:1–3.
43. See Matthew 21:28–32; Luke 15:11–24; Luke 18:9–14.
44. See John 3:16.
45. John A. Widtsoe, *Rational Theology* (Salt Lake City: General Priesthood Committee, 1915), 25.
46. See Matthew 1:20–23; John 1:14.
47. Jesus is referred to as "God" in all of the following New Testament verses: John 1:1, 18; John 20:28; Romans 9:5; Titus 2:13; Hebrews 1:8; 2 Peter 1:1.
48. See John 1:1; John 17:5; Colossians 1:15–17; Hebrews 1:3–4, 10–12.
49. See John 5:18; John 10:30–33.
50. The worship of Jesus began with his first disciples: see Matthew 14:33; Matthew 28:9, 17. One letter in the New Testament says that even the angels worship Jesus (see Hebrews 1:6)!
51. See Exodus 20:3–6; Exodus 34:14; Deuteronomy 6:13; Deuteronomy 8:19. Jesus reaffirmed this Old Testament teaching: see Matthew 4:10.
52. See Romans 1:25; Revelation 22:8–9.

# Subject Index

Abraham, 38, 67
agnosticism, 43
All-In-God Question, 31
All-Is-God Question, 30, 31
Atheism, 43, 62; as a minority view, 43
Atheist worldviews, 27, 43–44; challenges facing, 43–44; denial of any transcendent ordering of the universe, 47. *See also* Atheistic Dualism; Atheistic Idealism; Materialism
Atheistic Dualism, 55–56; challenges facing, 55–56
Atheistic Idealism, 57–58; advantage over Materialism, 57; challenges facing, 57–58

Baha'i Faith, as a religion, 100
Berkeley, George, 57
biases, 16
blind men and the elephant analogy, 24, 88
Buddhism, 81, 87; as a religion, 100

"Choose Your Own Adventure" (CYOA) books, 11; as "game books," 11; "interactive storyline" in, 11, 15
Christianity, 40, 59–60; challenges facing, 59–60; as a Monotheist worldview, 34; and the problem of evil, 59; as a religion, 100; view of God, 40, 59; view of heaven (as "eternal life") and hell (as "eternal death"), 40; view of Jesus, 36, 38, 39, 40, 51, 59, 87, 96–97
Church of Jesus Christ of Latter-day Saints. *See* Mormonism
Classical Theism, 36; view of God, 47
Codex Alexandrinus, 106n30
Codex Sinaiticus, 106n30
Communication Question, 34, 35
Confucianism, as a religion, 100

Deism, 61–62; challenges facing, 61–62; and the laws of physics, 61; popularity of among eighteenth- and nineteenth-century intellectuals, 62; and the problem of evil, 62; view of God (as a watchmaker), 61
Deuteronomy, book of: curses for Israel's failure to obey God's commandments in, 106n36; repeating of the requirement to keep the laws and commandments of God in, 106n35
divine revelation, 34, 35; in Christianity, 59; in Theist worldviews, 35
Divinity Question, 39
Dualism, 55

## Subject Index

evil, problem of: and Christianity, 59; and Deism, 62; and Finite Godism, 63–64; and Panentheism, 79–80; and Pantheism, 79–80, 81–82; and Theist worldviews, 45–46
evolution, 56, 58

Finite Godism, 63–64; challenges facing, 63–64; and the problem of evil, 63–64; view of God, 63
Finite Theism, 33, 49; view of God, 33
Finite Theist worldviews, 49–50; challenges facing, 49–50; view of God, 49. *See also* Finite Godism
free choices, 19, 20
Freedom Question, 19

God Question, 25, 27, 43, 55, 57
goodness, as godliness, 40, 45
Goodness Question, 23, 32, 40, 43, 44, 45, 70, 72, 81

Hare Krishna movement, 79
Hegel, G. W. F., 79
Hinduism, 79, 81; as a family of religions, 79; as a religion, 100; view of God, 87

Idealism, 57. *See also* Atheistic Idealism; Theistic Idealism
Ignatius of Antioch, 95–96
Islam, 65–66; challenges facing, 66; emphasis on the idea of law, 65; and the Hadith, 65; meaning of the word *Islam* ("submission" or "surrender"), 65; as a Monotheist worldview, 34, 65; and the Qur'an, 37, 65; as a religion, 100; view of God (Allah), 65; view of holy books, 65, 66, 106n25; view of Jesus, 38, 87; view of Muhammad (as the true prophet of God), 37, 38; view of paradise and hell, 65–66

Jainism, as a religion, 100
Jehovah's Witnesses, 101
Jesus, 38, 51, 60, 67–68, 83; as Christ, 106n31; as God, 95, 107n47; as the Messiah ("the Anointed One"), 67; resurrection of, 36, 51, 52, 67; worship of, 96, 107n50
Judaism, 67–68; challenges facing, 67–68; emphasis of modern Judaism on how a person lives rather than what he or she believes, 67; as a Monotheist worldview, 34; as a religion, 100; and the Talmud, 67; and the Tanach, 67; as a Theist worldview, 67; and the Torah, 38, 67; view of Abraham, 38, 67; view of God, 87; view of Jesus, 38, 68; view of Moses (as "the Father of the Prophets"), 38

King, Martin Luther, Jr., 102
Knowledge Question, 22, 72

Lewis, C. S., 14

Mao Tse-tung, 102
Materialism, 28, 57, 69–70; challenges facing, 69–70; influence of modern science on, 69; and the laws of physics, 69, 70, 107n38
Matter Question, 27, 28

# Subject Index

messianic prophecies, in the Old Testament, 67, 106n34
Mind Question, 28
Monism, 71–72, 81; challenges facing, 71–72; in Eastern philosophies and religions, 71; etymology of (Greek *monos,* "single" or "alone"), 71
Monotheist ("one God") worldviews, 34, 89–90. *See also* Christianity; Islam; Judaism
Mormonism, 101; as a Polytheist worldview, 89
Moses, 38, 67
Moses Question, 38
Muhammad, 37, 38, 65
Muhammad Question, 37
Mysticism, 73–74; challenges facing, 73–74; etymology of (Greek *musticon,* "secret"), 73; view of God, 73

Neo-Paganism, 81, 101
New Age movement, 81, 101
Nihilism, 44, 75–76; challenges facing, 75–76; etymology of (Latin *nihil,* "nothing"), 75
Non-Christian Theist worldviews, 51–52; view of Jesus, 51–52
Non-Mainstream Monotheism, 77–78; challenges facing, 77, 78; as a "minority report," 77–78; view of God, 77

Openness Question, 35

Panentheism, 79–80, 101; and Eastern religions, 79; etymology of (Greek *pan, en, theos,* "all-in-God"), 79; and the problem of evil, 79–80; view of God, 79–80

Pantheism, 79, 81–82, 101; in Eastern cultures, 81; etymology of (Greek *pan, theos,* "all-God"), 81; and the problem of evil, 79–80, 81–82; view of God, 79, 81
Parmenides, 26; on "the One," 26
Pelagianism, 83–84; condemnation of as heresy, 84
Pelagius, 83
Perfection Question, 32
person, 29
Personality Question, 29, 31, 61
Plato, 85
Platonism, 85–86; advantage over other worldviews, 85; challenges facing, 85–86; view of God, 85
Pliny the Younger, 39
Pluralism, 87–88; challenges facing, 87–88
Polytheism, 89–90; challenges facing, 89–90; etymology of (Greek *polus, theos,* "many gods"), 89; as a Finite Theist worldview, 89
prophet, 37; a true prophet of God, 37
Pyrrho, 93

Quasi-Theism, 47
Quasi-Theist worldviews, 30, 47–48; advantages over Atheism, 47; challenges facing, 47–48; as a sort of middle ground between Atheism and Classical Theism, 48; view of God, 47

Relativism, 91–92; challenges facing, 91–92; the Cultural Relativist, 91; the Subjectivist, 91

# Subject Index

religion, 100; definition of, 100; the difference between a religion and a worldview, 100; diversity of, 24
Religion Question, 24
Resurrection Question, 36

Salvation Question, 40
Sikhism, as a religion, 100
Skepticism, 93–94; challenges facing, 93–94
solipsism, 58
Spinoza, Baruch, 30; on *Deus sive Natura* ("God or Nature"), 30

Taoism, 81
Theism, 45
Theist worldviews, 29, 32, 45–46, 64; differences between Theist worldviews, 29, 45; and divine revelation, 35; and the problem of evil, 45–46; view of God, 29, 32, 85–86; view of Jesus, 36. *See also* Classical Theism; Finite Theism
Theistic Idealism, 57
things, categories of: material things, 27; mental things, 27, 28
Tolkien, J. R. R., 14
truth: as objective, 21; as relative, 21
Truth Question, 21, 32, 72

Uniqueness Question, 33
Unitarianism, 95–96; challenges facing, 95–96; rejection of the doctrines of the Trinity and the incarnation, 95; view of God, 95
Unity Question, 26, 27, 72
universe, 30; design of, 47; relationship between the universe and God, 30, 31

value judgments, 23, 76

Watchtower Society. *See* Jehovah's Witnesses
Widtsoe, John A., 89
worldview: changing one's worldview, 14; definition of, 12, 100; the difference between a worldview and a religion, 100; how your worldview affects the way you see things, 13; as indispensable for thinking, 12; and people's opinions on matters of ethics and politics, 13; as a philosophical view of the world, 12; things you can do to deepen your understanding of your worldview, 97–98; why your worldview matters, 102